EATING GOD

A Book of
BHAKTI POETRY

EATING GOD

EDITED AND WITH AN
INTRODUCTION BY

ARUNDHATHI
SUBRAMANIAM

PENGUIN
ANANDA

An imprint of Penguin Random House

PENGUIN ANANDA

USA | Canada | UK | Ireland | Australia
New Zealand | India | South Africa | China | Singapore

Penguin Ananda is part of the Penguin Random House group of companies
whose addresses can be found at global.penguinrandomhouse.com

Published by Penguin Random House India Pvt. Ltd
4th Floor, Capital Tower 1, MG Road,
Gurugram 122 002, Haryana, India

Penguin
Random House
India

First published in Penguin Ananda by Penguin Books India 2014

10 9 8 7 6 5 4 3 2

ISBN 9780670087594

Typeset in Aldine401 BT by R. Ajith Kumar, New Delhi
Printed at Replika Press Pvt. Ltd, India

www.penguin.co.in

This is a legitimate digitally printed version of the book and therefore might not
have certain extra finishing on the cover.

Contents

Contents

Contents

Contents

Introduction

There are poems, and there are poems.

There are poems that get under your skin and seep into your marrow without your even realizing you have been annexed. There are poems that become a part of the aural backdrop of your inner life, hypnotic and resonant. There are poems that tease the human cortex so that each reading becomes a decoding, an unravelling.

And then there are poems that assault you in some unknown part of your inner geography. A place both mysterious and familiar. A place that you recognize as a dark place of origin, marking the beginnings of an ancient human ache. A place that has sometimes been called the heart, sometimes the soul, and, by the doggedly unsentimental, the gut.

This is the breath-catching moment when self speaks to self more directly than you ever thought possible. A moment that sears through the smog of belief and doctrine, the endlessly recycled traffic of theology, the air waves of opinion. A moment when you know you are witness to the self pretending to be none other than itself—a simple, insatiable throb. This is a throb that will not be silenced. This is a throb that will not settle for bucket list petitions, for easy deals with a brokering god.

This is a throb that demands everything—all that ever was and ever will be, all that is here and now, and all that is before and beyond. It clamours for form and for no form, for thingy-ness and for no-thingness, even perhaps while knowing all along that there is not much difference between the two.

This is a throb so definitive, so encompassing that it blurs the conventional divide between the sacred and the profane. It is a throb that demands union and annihilation, love and liberation, ecstasy and extinction, more and no more—and demands it now.

Everyone has known it. Many choose to forget, defer, deny or dilute it. Understandably. It is inconvenient. It makes life difficult. When one does encounter it, however, one knows one is in the presence of something fragile, urgent, moltenly alive.

This is bhakti.

And this sharp text message to the human epicentre, this bruising and yet exhilarating arrow to the core of one's being—this is the province of Bhakti poetry.

꽃

Experientially, the condition is as old as time. Historically, the movement had its identifiable moment of emergence on the Indian subcontinent—an exuberant birthing that assumed the proportions of a tidal wave that crashed across the great barrier reefs of region and language, caste and class. The poet, scholar and preeminent Bhakti poetry translator A.K. Ramanujan described it as the 'great many-sided shift [that] occurred in Hindu culture and sensibility between the sixth and ninth centuries'. Bhakti, he says, 'is one name for that shift'.

Sacred texts like the Bhagavad Gita and strands of Upanishadic literature had invoked it earlier. But Bhakti, as a series of popular cults, celebrating devotion as the supreme road to the divine, began taking shape around the eighth century. The historical reasons for its emergence in diverse regions are varied—ranging from the rigidity of Brahminism to the need to carve out a spiritual identity vitalized by, and yet distinct from, the Shramana movements, and, later, Islam—and it is not the intention of this book to dwell on the complex factors shaping its chronology.

It is clear, however, that the movement was not unitary. The regional cults were divergent in belief and practice. The objects of devotion were the gods, Shiva and Vishnu, in embodied and non-figurative versions, as well as the goddess or Devi in her many manifestations. But it is clear that these regional upsurges did not evolve 'out of some original teaching or spread through conversion' (as historian Romila Thapar points out). Instead, they surfaced across a period of a thousand years when historical circumstances were ripe for their emergence, converging with the growing need of lower castes to give voice to their aspirations.

Sanskrit, that venerable matriarch of several Indian

languages, had held monarchs and metaphysicians in her thrall for centuries. The sacred traditions of revelation (*sruti*) and recollection (*smriti*) were already known to comprise a rich heritage of spiritual literature. And yet, for all her lapidary refinement, her exquisite subtlety, Sanskrit gradually began to seem inadequate to meet the needs of a growing tribe of spiritual aspirants. This new tribe comprised men and women, seized by a collective feverish thirst. They were potters and peasants, weavers and cobblers, basket-makers and palanquin-bearers, musicians and milkmen, scholars and tax-collectors, boatmen and blacksmiths, pundits and hangmen, pariahs and priests, plebeians and princesses.

What did they have in common? Nothing, seemingly. Except for the fact that they dared to give voice to their longing. They were incendiary dreamers who refused to be mere worshippers, anarchic visionaries who refused to be mere inheritors. They were less god-fearing than god-possessed, less content to receive an ancient wisdom than impatient to express their own tempestuous interiority. It was a strange condition, this bhakti, this unappeasable lust, this clamorous yearning, this greed.

And so, the bhakta was born—a new and colourful figure on the Indian spiritual landscape, wild and incorrigible, unquenchable in his yearning, irrepressible in his authenticity. With his cussed insistence on singing the dialect of his heart—its lurching passions and plummeting despairs—he became the voice of a people, the leader of a community, an embodiment of the zeitgeist. In his poems, he sang and lamented, cursed and celebrated, hungered and praised, loudly, lustily, sometimes embarrassingly. And he never stopped demanding.

What did he demand? Nothing less than the divine—the glorious, unmediated divine. And what's more, he seemed to see evidence of divinity everywhere. He saw it in the ordinary life ordinarily lived. He saw it in life's detritus and trivia—in cloth and clay, in pots and pans, in the temple and on the street, in the grandeur of the scriptures and in his own robust demotic. He exulted when he saw it and despaired when he lost sight of it; he yearned to devour it and be devoured by it; he sought it in the world of throbbing materiality and he sought it in the shadowy provinces beyond the threshold of the senses.

'A bhakta,' as A.K. Ramanujan says, 'is not content to worship a god in word and ritual, nor is he content to grasp him in a theology; he needs to possess him and be possessed by him. He also needs to sing, to dance, to make poetry, painting, shrines, sculpture; to embody him in every possible way.'

It was a relationship of such intimacy that it made every tone permissible—rebuke, banter, humour, lust, entreaty, indignation, rage. God was sublime, exalted, beautiful, but he was also family. He could be addressed the way one might speak to a beloved, if habitually disobedient, member of one's household. And the only means to speak to such a god was in the homespun cadences of the vernacular, which seemed to come closest (even if never close enough) to the many shifts of the bhakta's inner weather. Sanskrit—and indeed any standardized language, whether courtly or regional—seemed too remote to suit this hot, spluttering, sometimes inarticulate dialogue conducted in the innermost chamber of the heart.

Sanskrit was never entirely erased. Several poets acknowledged their debt to it. Several drew from its vocabulary, but at the same time further nourished their regional languages with the flavour of local dialects, to create a new idiom of striking contrasts and verbal textures. Even while Tamil poets like Appar sang the praises of Tamil and proclaimed the equality of their verse to Vedic scripture, they weren't simply resorting to an easy chauvinism.

The bhaktas' impatience was, instead, with everything that seemed frozen and straitjacketed. Into stone as into language, these poets sought to breathe life. They demanded a divinity and a diction that was spontaneous, responsive, alert to their needs—fiery, riverine, untamable. They sought a tongue that could be sacred without ceasing to be earthy, a god who could be human without ceasing to be divine, domestic without ceasing to be cosmic, and a path that could be particular, popular, and even profane, without ceasing to be a pilgrimage. With the scorching white heat of their words they consecrated the lowly and the inconsequential, the humble ghettos and dark enclaves of human experience, proving that every by-lane, every forgotten alleyway of language, locality and life could be just another way home.

It is tempting to see this as a sudden rupture in the fabric of time. But dramatic though it was, Bhakti was not quite as estranged from the past or its immediate context as it might seem. There were parallel strains and impulses—the esoteric traditions of Tantra and Yoga as well as the impact of Sufi mysticism—that cast their influence on the Bhakti movement and were, in turn, enriched by it. Besides, as historians remind us, even as it rejected aspects of tradition, Bhakti also imbibed from the past. And yet, even while it absorbed, it subverted and redefined.

The movement—or series of movements, as some prefer to see it—had its beginnings in South India in the Tamil regional cults devoted to the gods Shiva and Vishnu. This was not surprising. Tamil had a literary tradition of considerable antiquity with its distinct classical as well as oral and folk avatars. And so the charged paeans in praise of Shiva (sung by the saint-poets called the Nayanmar) and the lyrical-erotic hymns in love of Vishnu (authored by the bard-devotees called the Alvar) captured the popular imagination in a new and powerful way. As these poets wandered the Tamil countryside with their ever-burgeoning tribe of followers, they infused all that they encountered with their poetry of incandescent love and sacred delirium, ensuring that no crevice in their inner or outer landscape remained god-forsaken. Why couldn't the Lord who dwelt in Kailash also reside in the Kaveri delta, asked the Nayanmar. Surely Shiva was too full of grace, too compassionate, too big to be contained in a single abode?

This inspired mayhem of lust for the divine could not be contained either. It spread from south to west, north to east, and by the sixteenth and seventeenth centuries had permeated the farthest reaches of the subcontinent. Regional and yet inter-regional, this participatory spiritual ethos grew widespread, holding out the possibility of mukti or liberation for all, asserting time and again that there was a path to the divine from exactly where one stood. For each and every flawed, humble, wondering human being, with her personal and collective freight of memory and aspiration, there was a way—a very singular way. You qualified by being human.

Bhakti—as this raging thirst for firsthand experience over secondhand knowledge came to be known—had certain similarities in its avatars across the subcontinent. Bhaktas of different provinces, backgrounds and sectarian allegiances seemed united in their adoption of a vigorous, inventive, often colloquial language; their rejection of traditional caste-bound social hierarchy; their impatience with superstition, ceremony, punditry and other traditional forms of intercession; their fierce assertion of their right to a personal and direct relationship with divinity; their avowed return to the 'original inspiration' of the ancient traditions (before the appropriation of the sacred by a clerical and academic elite); their affirmation of an identity distinct from the orthodoxies of Hinduism, Buddhism, Jainism and Islam (even while they absorbed and reinvigorated the legacies of these traditions); and their endorsement of a new fellowship based on spiritual attainment rather than social ascription.

Bhakti saints, as A.K. Ramanujan says, 'have been called the "great integrators", bringing the high to the low, esoteric paradox to the man in the street, transmuting ancient and abstruse ideas into live contemporary experience; at the same time, finding everyday symbols for the timeless.'

However, the devotional upsurge was far from uniform

and was veined with regional and historical variations. Early Tamil bhakti, for instance, seems to have been more accommodating of ritual and temple worship, less anti-Brahmin than its later counterparts. However, even here, as scholar-translator Indira Viswanathan Peterson points out, there was a subversive emphasis on integrity of intent. The devotees reinstated the true meaning of ritual by freeing it from mechanical habit and vulgar appeasement. They brought to it the high-voltage fervour of true yearning.

Another crucial variation was based on the espousal of *nirguna* or *saguna* bhakti—whether a devotee conceived of god as formless and impersonal or as embodied and personal. The former conception was shaped, no doubt, by Vedantin ideas as well as Sufism, with bhaktas like Kabir repudiating both Hindu and Muslim orthodoxies and others like Nanak pointing to a divinity without referring to the conceptions of either faith. Over time, much venom was spewed by apologists on either side of the divide, much contempt heaped, spleen vented. Texts were erased, edited, revised, doctored (as poet and Kabir translator Vinay Dharwadker explains) to suit the viewpoint of one or the other competing sect.

Much of the rant may seem, of course, irrelevant for contemporary readers who usually turn to Bhakti literature for the poet's voice—volatile, expressive, yearning, entreating, peremptory, despairing, and ecstatic—rather than the perfections of the god it describes. The subject of this poetry often seems, in fact, far more vivid and compelling than its object. Besides, the poet in both forms of bhakti asserts a personal devotion, without an intercessor. And so Tukaram's yearning for a flesh-and-blood Vithoba, for instance, has a distinct kinship in terms of tenor with a nirguna poet's commitment to a divinity beyond attributes. The originality and unconventionality of poets on both sides is in obvious evidence. As poet and translator Dilip Chitre says of Tukaram and his ferocious saguna bhakti: 'he is an image-worshipping iconoclast; … a sensuous ascetic; … an intense bhakta who would not hesitate to destroy his God out of sheer love.' Clearly, this kind of anarchic passion is not so different from the fearless dispassion of Kabir, so often held up as the unswerving champion of nirguna bhakti.

For all its vitality and radiance, the Bhakti movement was not without its contradictions. Its sometimes aggressive proselytizing zeal spawned its own forms of crude propaganda and bigotry. Besides, some of its rebellion seems to have remained theoretical. The challenge to caste was clearly not radical or enduring enough, and sometimes remained limited to the ideological rather than the material realm. Ironically, some of the most vehement iconoclasts of the movement were later canonized and domesticated by the very establishments against which they had dissented. There are also traces of misogyny and a puritanical rejection of the flesh in some of these poems.

And yet, the spirit of the movement, perhaps at times in spite of itself, was egalitarian. Whenever the experiential dimension overtook the doctrinal, as it often did, the poetry was charged with the resonance of freedom. Divine grace was seen as not just impartial; it was seen as indiscriminate—in fact, extravagantly democratic. The lord was no longer a distant promise, imprisoned in stone, incarcerated in theory, gridlocked in transcendent eternalism. The temple doors had swung open. Whispered arcana could now be proclaimed, sung, danced, shared. God was liberated at last.

They tumbled out in a festive cascade—gods and goddesses who were now free to saunter in and out of hearts at will. They could sulk when neglected, be wooed when peeved, be reprimanded when capricious. And they never ceased to be lovable, for they wept with the dispossessed and celebrated with the joyous. They understood lapses in attention and errors in grammar. They enjoyed trivia, relished detail and local gossip, revelled in the particular, had no ideological issues with the concrete. You didn't have to know their language; they already knew yours. You didn't have to propitiate them with a cargo of coconuts and terror; they were simply waiting for an invitation into your heart. They responded to sincerity and to love wherever they saw it. They weren't snobs.

And even for those bhaktas who saw god as unnameable and beyond personality, this was not a divinity shuttered in doctrine, swathed in esoteric wisdom. This was a presence that was unmistakably alive and immediate, pulsatingly now. No one could manipulate it, no one monopolize it, no one miss it.

This anthology is an invitation to listen to some of these poems of urgent love and impassioned unreason. These are poems that have permeated the collective unconscious of centuries of Indians, poems that comprise some of the timeless demotic literature of the subcontinent. Many of these poets were individuals recorded in history, but most of them have since been morphed into myth, beatified into sainthood, transformed into tradition. It is often difficult to tell which poems were authored by the individual and which by the many oral traditions they left in their wake. The voices in these poems, however, whether authored by one individual or many, are strongly, almost savagely, personal.

Most of these poems strike one with their emotional immediacy, their raw desire, and their vulnerable admissions of doubt, fear and uncertainty. There are others that remind you that poetry is the province of mystery, that you are now in a realm closer to mantra rather than manifesto; dreamtime rather than didacticism; song rather than sermon. Some are in a mode that has come to be known as 'twilight language' or *sandhyabhasha*, a dense, coded, elliptical language that shatters conventional notions of causality and daytime perception.

Here is a chance to tune into these sacred pop songs—from the bracing irony of Kabir, the weaver, to the wild abandon of Mirabai, the Rajput princess; from the distilled clarity of Lal Ded in Kashmiri to the audacious sensuality of Annamayya in Telugu; from the cannibalistic lust of the great Tamil Vaishnava saint Nammalvar to the uncompromising integrity and protestant ethos of Basavanna in Kannada; from the earthy mysticism of Tukaram in Marathi to the fiery eroticism of Chandidas in Bengali.

These are voices that readers have probably encountered before. But this selection is an invitation to hear them in a great melodic chorus, in the magic of polyphony. The channels are deliberately mixed. The arrangement is not chronological, sectarian or linguistic. The specific social, doctrinal and literary contexts of these poems are certainly important.

But there are several books that have already explored these regional and individual timbres. What this volume offers is instead a chance to hear these voices in unison—as a single soaring octave of human longing and freedom.

Abandoning a schematic editorial approach, this anthology positions each poem in an aural mosaic based on tone and texture. There are lust poems, rage poems, raging thirst poems, wistful poems, erotic poems, funny poems, ecstatic poems, ironic poems, doubting poems, adoring poems, anguished poems, protest poems, celebratory poems, the whole gamut. The gestalt, one hopes, will make for a varied and yet cohesive listening experience.

This is as much a book of poems as it is a map of the existential journey. It is intended as much for lovers of poetry as it is for seekers across the board. Above all, this collection attempts to offer the flavour of an epoch—the foam and brine of an oceanic explosion of yearning, when men and women spilled out of their social definitions and gods and goddesses spilled out of shrines and scripture, and the two met in a tantalizing duet of seeking and finding, touching and losing, glimpsing and forgetting, that has never been seen before or since on this scale in the history of this subcontinent, and perhaps the world.

Empowered by the Bhakti poets who used the first person singular without apology, it is time to implicate my own role in this project. I do not consider myself a scholar in the field.

I am, however, a seasoned listener and lover of poetry, and I share with these poets a deep conviction in the power of the word, when it is born of heightened states of consciousness, to transfigure. Not all these poems embody blazingly obvious literary merit. While some of these poems do experiment with idiom and prosody, and some even invented new forms and interrogated traditional notions of poetry, others are relatively simple lyrics, waiting to be released into the landscape of song. Almost all of them *were* sung. And yet, if even the written words are capable of creating inner tectonic shifts it is because they were fashioned in places of extraordinary ferment.

My fascination with these poems stems from the fact that I know something of the condition of the upstart seeker, the amateur flounderer. And I know the experience of the sometimes desperate devotee. At times when my own journey has seemed scarily unmapped, it is to some of the churning Marathi *abhangas* of Tukaram and Namdev, to Ramanujan's glorious translations of Nammalvar, to Pandit Kumar Gandharva's inimitable vocal renditions of Kabir, that I have turned. And it is in those hoarse, unvarnished words that I found my campfire, a dim outline of community. It was in those fractured silences that I found, however fleetingly, my satsangh. Later, when ambushed by that cyclone of dark joy and bewilderment, which is how I experienced my encounter with a spiritual guide, I realized that bhakti isn't just starry-eyed song and comfort food. It is, above all, the deep science of the heart.

The divide between nirguna and saguna bhakti, despite its heritage of sectarian tensions, poses no real barrier to the omnivorous seeker. Devotion, as followers of all spiritual traditions realize at some point, is merely a *device,* a means to fuel the spiritual quest. It is the experience of bhakti that transforms, rather than its content. One senses how the notion of a formless divine could be a valuable means to check the obsessive literalism of some votaries of saguna bhakti. Equally, the god with name, shape and form (not to mention consort, constitution, family history and preferred choice of vehicle) is a wonderful means to counter the sterile metaphysical strain among some nirguna dogmatists.

What is particularly interesting in these poems is the way devotion is often suffused with eroticism. The fervour of bhakti shot through with *shringara*, or sexual love, comprises, in fact, some of the richest poetry in the genre. Velcheru Narayana Rao and David Shulman have pointed out how the fifteenth-century Telugu poet Annamacharya's metaphysical or introspective poems seem to emerge from the same 'inner space' as his erotic poems. The former, written in the male mode, has a voice that is troubled, tormented and conflicted; the latter, written in the female mode, has a voice that is far more confident and relaxed in its bold and playful sensuality. Eroticism here is not just courtly or romantic love; spiritual hunger is not just pasteurized asexual longing. One leaks into the other, and together both 'articulate a wide range of human experience' that is never monochromatic, never anaemic. It is a reminder of how inextricably linked the sexual is to the spiritual, the physical to the metaphysical. It is also a reminder of a fact familiar to every poet: that there is no way to articulate subtler areas of experience except in sensuous terms.

At first glance, it is possible to feel somewhat discomfited at the seemingly pat gender roles in some of these poems: passive female devotee, dynamic male god. But as you look deeper, you find these are enlivened and undercut in all kinds of ways, with power equations fluctuating crazily the closer you get to the rising temperature of the bedchamber. The 'female' devotee is no demure bride; she is capable of tying her lover's arms to the bedpost (Narsinh Mehta), kicking him out of bed (Salabega), imperiously designating him her slave (Annamacharya). And god, as we see in Jayadeva and so many others, pines for his beloved in a way that can be pathetic and heart-rending; he is both creditor and debtor, conqueror and conquered, raider and raided, capricious boss and humble slave. And he even shows an occasional propensity for cross-dressing, to add an exciting twist to the recipe.

I find myself drawn by the resolute absence of sentimentalism in these poems. The bhaktas here are feral. They are willing to wreck homes and marriages, commit adultery and suicide, turn homicidal and cannibalistic with impunity, as long as it brings them closer to the objects of their desire. 'Take these husbands who die,/ decay, and feed them/ to your kitchen fires!' cries Akka Mahadevi with breathtaking brutality. Nammalvar warns his god of his intention even more plainly: 'If I see you anywhere/ I'll gather you/ and eat you up.'

To live in these seismic zones, then, is to live in the knowledge that intimacy can be alarmingly disruptive, turning hierarchies into states of hectic disarray. The irreverence is rooted in the deep recognition that the lover and the beloved cannot be separated for long, however hard they try. The union is only a matter of time. And so, it is possible to reproach a god, hurl the choicest cuss words at him, personalize him, infantilize him, cannibalize him, knowing all along that he is the sustainer of life and the world. 'Just calling a large thing small.../ does not diminish its size,' says the poet Rahim. 'Krishna, who lifted the vast mount Govardhan/ won't take it amiss if called Murlidhar.'

The body remains a recurrent and important presence in these poems; interestingly, it is not denied, wished away, or spiritualized into bloodlessness. We are told time and again that there is more to us than flesh and bone. 'That pampered carcass/ believes maya to be his friend./ But maya will chew him down/ to his entrails,' says Akho in no uncertain terms. All the poets reiterate that theme of material perishability in their own ways. But the body is also the locus of wisdom, an instrument of knowing. 'Man is the greatest Truth/ of all,/ Nothing beyond,' proclaims Chandidas, supremely confident that his declaration in no way contradicts his love of Krishna. For the body is, above all, a shrine, worthy of being the sanctum for the greatest mystery of all. The moving temples are the ones that last, says Basavanna in what is one of the justifiably most famous poems in the vachana tradition. 'If menstrual blood makes me impure/ Tell me who was not born of that blood,' asks a fearless Soyarabai. And Devara Dasimayya, the weaver, rebukes God for creating the body and then enjoining its transcendence: 'Just once/ Take on a body like mine/ And see for yourself, O Ramanatha.'

These poems also remind us that the paths of devotion

and knowledge are not mutually exclusive. They reaffirm that no human being is just a bhakta or a *jnana margi*, a devotee or a savant. Devotion, for all its seeming unreasonableness, I have grown to understand over the years, has its own deep intelligence. Likewise, the most discerning intellectual enquiry is empty without the lubrication of passion. Reading many of these saint-poets is a reminder that bhakti is not (as so many believe) a state of imbecilic joy or emotional jingoism. There are several instances in these poems of psychological complexity—nuances, darker subtexts, sudden humour, a startling carnality. All these moments testify to the fact that the bhakta was not a beaming saint with a calendar art halo. She was instead an insurgent who knew the perils of the border game she was playing, and the yawning chasm that lay just beyond the horizon of her insatiable yearning.

There can be no knowing without love and no love without logic. In a world that splinters idea and emotion, mind and body, faith and reason, into easy binaries, this essential synthesis is often forgotten. When Abhirami Bhattar gives us the striking image of Devi's breasts searing Shiva's chest—'But you/ you scarred/ this warrior's body/ with your breasts,/ great Goddess'—he integrates seeming incongruities in a single metaphor. We are reminded in one stroke that fragility is not without power, subtlety is not without strength, love is not without wisdom. The poet Surdas's lines jolt us into a similar state of recognition, as he underscores the need to forego a glib intellectualism in order to uncover a deeper vision:'For who has ever recognized the brilliance of the sun/ but by seeing it through eyes gone blind?' Likewise Lalon Fakir implores us to awaken to the dangers of a barren, self-serving rationality before it is too late: 'Or else/ You'll die/ A useless death/ Bailing out/ Water with a thimble.'

For any reader who has known some of the peaks and troughs of the human spiritual cardiogram, Bhakti poetry brings its own very particular rewards. The poems offer sanctuary, companionship, illumination—signposts on what often is a turbulent and uncertain journey. They are reminders of the human struggle to give utterance to that strange hunger for something that we seem perennially on the verge of apprehending—the mystery that, in Mircea Eliade's words, is 'totally foreign to us, but [with which] we are completely at home'; the intimate tug towards something so familiar that it could be mother, father, lover, child, teacher, master, and yet obstinately more, much more, than the sum of all those roles.

What continues to inspire me about these poems is that they tell us that even at all those times when we felt homeless, desolate, dislocated or despairing, we were not abandoned. They remind us that the gnawing human experience of distance or *viraha* from the deeper mysteries of life need not be a cause for despair. There can be no harvest without fallowness, they tell us. No experience of separation, however arid, they say, is ever devoid of presence or grace. Waiting is not mere passivity; it can be a state of dynamic receptivity, a radical and alive responsiveness. God lurks even in the condition of exile, says Akka Mahadevi, in her memorable image of 'the Brahman hiding in yearning'. For Tukaram, every crisis can be seen as a visiting card from the divine: 'When He comes/ Out of the blue/ A meteorite/ Shattering your home/ Be sure/ God is visiting you,' he says in what I consider to be my talismanic poem in the book.

For all its ordeals and trials, the journey can offer, through the alchemy of love, moments as exhilarating as the destination. And at times, evidently, there is not much difference between the two. These poems remind us—time and time again—to enjoy the ride. For if there's one thing that is not in short supply, it is grace: 'I lost myself in myself and found a wine cellar… jars and jars of the good stuff,' exults Lal Ded. 'Blue is one's Guru and one's Guru's resort/ I behave blue I feed on blue/ I become blue I envision blue,' exclaims a dazed Jnaneshwar. 'He is reaching the brim now! In an instant, He is going to overflow!' declares Tukaram, lost in a surplus of drunken ecstasy.

This book invites you to sit back and drink in that abundance.

A Note on the Selections

Making an anthology is a chastening business. You start out with a blueprint for a yacht, sleek and streamlined. You end up with an ark. Only to discover that you're no Noah. You play host, it is true, and you're honoured by all the fauna that choose to grace your boat. But most of the time you're a wide-eyed mariner, awed by the capacity of life to love, to yearn, to sing through a blue chaos of water and an infinitude of sky.

The animals on board this vessel come in varied stripes and persuasions. The dream was to accommodate as many as there are; the reality is necessarily more circumscribed. In the sea of Bhakti literature, this ark is a coracle. But I like to believe it is a large-hearted coracle, inclusive in spirit, in its approach to the ancient business of stargazing, its willingness to sacrifice a tidiness of line for a more leaky-tub hospitality.

And yes, the attempt was to open the doors to god-crazed poets from as many regions, languages and temperaments as possible, poets of diverse cultural backgrounds, genders and faith contexts. To welcome all divinities—those who carry flutes and those who wear crescent moons, to make room for gods and for goddesses with a staggering variety of names and addresses, for those who wear form and those who have thrown off all figurative attire. Which is why the book swelled to a size so much larger than I or the publisher had originally envisaged.

But above all, the idea was to travel the serrated emotional arc of bhakti—from wild longing through fury, despair, love, laughter, rapture and lunacy towards heady liberation. It is an arc that seekers recognize, even if they haven't reached the end of their journeys yet. And it is an arc that assures us that the radiance of song can be carried into every dank and festering crevice of human consciousness. And so, any simple arithmetic about featuring a fixed number of poems from a fixed number of poets and languages seemed out of place. The overriding editorial criterion in this volume was *tone*—finding poems that spoke in diverse, compelling, even contrary ways, about the human thirst for freedom.

You will find well-known poets in here, and lesser-known ones, and in varying ratios; much-loved poems and less familiar ones; previously published poems and unpublished ones; buoyantly free translations and stoutly faithful ones; formal registers and slangy ones; metrical forms and supple shape-shifting ones. The approaches to translation are as varied as the translators, but each has its own inherent logic and integrity. And the poems that eventually made their way in here are those that work as poems, that show signs of being context-sensitive and yet creative; respectful of the challenges encountered in utterances shaped by other worldviews and yet alive to the demands of modern literary form.

A.K. Ramanujan's translations of the Kannada vachana poets are here—a tribute to some of the richest works of modern Bhakti translation—alongside Dilip Chitre's passionate renditions of Tukaram and Linda Hess and Shukdev Singh's stirring translations of Kabir. But the book also acknowledges more recent volumes that have extended and inflected the scope of translation in their own ways, V. Narayana Rao and David Shulman's sumptuous edition of Annamacharya being chief among them. H.S. Shivaprakash on the Kannada poets, Indira Viswanathan Peterson on the Tamil Shaiva bards, Archana Venkatesan's work on the Tamil Vaishnava mystics, as well as John Stratton Hawley and Mark Juergensmeyer on the North Indian saint-poets, have nourished this book in vital ways. There were also several happy discoveries I made along the way: Deben Bhattacharya's moving translations of Vidyapati and Chandidas, for instance, or Dilip Chitre's unpublished manuscript of the Marathi *sant kavis*.

I am particularly interested in the translation ventures upon which contemporary Indian fellow poets have embarked. These include recent volumes by Vinay Dharwadker and Arvind Krishna Mehrotra on Kabir, as also Ranjit Hoskote's book on Lal Ded. This book also integrates work from ongoing projects in interesting states of creative ferment, such as Gieve Patel's long-standing, as yet unpublished work on Akho. More recent works in progress include Ravi Shankar and Priya Sarukkai Chabria's translations of Andal, and Jerry Pinto and Neela Bhagwat's of some of the lesser-known Marathi women mystics.

I was delighted by those poets who volunteered with enthusiasm to undertake translations for the purpose of this anthology: Rahul Soni, Mustansir Dalvi, Keki Daruwalla with Meena Desai, Anand Thakore, Sampurna Chattarji, Amit Chaudhuri, Prabhanjan Mishra, Mohan Gehani with Menka Shivdasani, are among these. I also learnt from some of these poets in the course of a correspondence that lasted several months and sometimes years, how this work extended them in various ways. In some cases I believe these brief trysts have triggered long-term commitments. So it is cheering to know a few books on individual Bhakti poets are likely to emerge as a consequence of this project. My own curiosity about the eighteenth-century Tamil text, the *Abhirami Antadi,* would never have deepened had it not been for this project. An abiding personal fascination with the Devi was, of course, the deeper impetus.

Chronologically, the poems in this volume date from the eighth century to the eighteenth. This wide and churning crucible of voices collectively comprise what has come to be known as the Bhakti literary heritage of this country. It was tempting to include modern and even contemporary poetry, which has been shaped by this counter-cultural legacy. But I eventually decided to relinquish that idea because the intricate network of tributaries and distributaries it opened up in each language seemed to call for an independent volume altogether.

I also grappled initially with questions about where to draw lines of demarcation, particularly given the porous membranes that separate Sufi and Bhakti literature. It is now clear to me that only an autonomous Sufi poetry anthology can do justice to the many poets in that tradition. At the same time, I enjoyed the blurring of lines that figures like Guru Nanak, Kabir, Lalon Fakir, Rahim, Salabega and Sami brought with them—reminders that the great democracy of human idea and feeling cannot be contained in narrow gated communities. The rest of the poets can be viewed as belonging more traditionally within the fold of Bhakti poetry, which is, in any case, an incredibly diverse and complex one. Several of them are still unfamiliar to contemporary lay readers and deserve a wider hearing in English translation.

What is lost in translation? To say a great deal, is a truism. These poems have been preserved for centuries through the oral tradition, and almost all are meant to be sung. On any page, in any language, in English or otherwise, the magic of music with its swoop and soar and careen is lost. On the other hand, something could well be gained—a wider readership perhaps inclined to approach some of the original songs with a renewed curiosity. This is where the value of translation lies. Besides, poetry as a *spoken* utterance, in any language, has its own alchemy. Several of these translations can be spoken aloud, savoured as epigram, tasted as chemical compounds (of varying pH values).

One might argue that some of the translators are primarily interested in these poems as literary artefacts rather than sacred utterances. While I have selected those translations where one approach hasn't snuffed out another, I believe there is, in any case, image and resonance enough in these poems, not to mention a deep tearing hunger, that fractures the creamiest of lines. The Bhakti poets make sure they get heard. There is no doubt about that. Their songs, even in translation, work as poetry does—as infection, not ideology, as contagion, not conviction.

The title of the volume is inspired by a poem by Nammalvar, that remarkable Tamil Vaishnava mystic, translated by A.K. Ramanujan—a reminder that the journey of bhakti, despite its intermittent disparagement of the flesh, is, in essence, as earthy as it is existential, as visceral as it is sacred, as human as it is divine.

A caveat. While there are voices here from all kinds of places—geographical, social, linguistic, psychological, historical—this is not a comprehensive Bhakti almanac. There are hundreds of poets who are not in these pages for various reasons, ranging from the fact that they haven't been translated to the fact that there simply wasn't room for indefinite expansion. In any case, this was never intended to be about zonal representation. This book is excited about cultural diversity, but it is not a cultural enterprise. It is excited about the trajectories of interest followed by contemporary Indian poets, but it is not just a literary enterprise.

The driving force of this book lies elsewhere. It is a book of sacred poems, where 'sacred' is the operative word. This makes it, essentially, a book for those who thirst. It is for those who recognize that bhakti for all its specificity has nothing, at heart, to do with dogmas of gender, caste, region or creed. It is for those who are willing to allow that human beings are about matter as well as spirit, that the 'this-worldly' and the 'other-worldly' are not necessarily at loggerheads.

The poems in here are unique and singular. They are also porous and permeable. It is true that, as readers, we cannot blithely appoint ourselves modern-day Akka Mahadevis and Tukarams; there may be unbridgeable impasses of context, not to mention spiritual delusions of grandeur in such assumptions. At the same time, we needn't be wary of claiming these poets as our relatives. If we feel drawn to their ever-widening embrace, it is because of the tug of old blood ties. They are *us*—as lost, as loving, as desperate as we can be, even if they seem to sustain it on another voltage at times. It is time to rescue them from sanctified specimenhood, to claim them not as creaky ancestors, but as part of our widening fellowship of the heart. They are our true genealogy.

An ark ostensibly offers refuge, but for much of its making, the inhabitants of this ark have been *my* refuge, providing me with varying doses of anchorage and awakening. I trust that they will offer the same to visiting shoals of fellow readers.

'ONLY SOMEONE STRUCK BY IT KNOWS THE PAIN'

That Strange Disease Called Bhakti

Don't you take on
this thing called bhakti:

> like a saw
> it cuts when it goes
>
> and it cuts again
> when it comes.

If you risk your hand
with a cobra in a pitcher
will it let you
pass?

(Basavanna: A.K. Ramanujan)

Like a sharp arrow
    Is the love of Rama.
Only someone struck by it
    Knows the pain.

You look for the wound,
    But the skin is not broken.
You bring out the ointment,
    But there's nowhere to rub.

When all women
    Look the same,
Who among them
    Will the lord choose?

Fortunate is she,
    Says Kabir,
In the parting of whose hair,
    And hers alone,

Is put vermilion.

(Kabir: A.K. Mehrotra)

Better than meeting
and mating all the time
is the pleasure of mating once
after being far apart.

When he's away
I cannot wait
to get a glimpse of Him.

Friend, when will I have it
both ways,
be with Him
yet not with Him,
my lord white as jasmine?

(Akka Mahadevi: A.K. Ramanujan)

Out of his desolate jungle cave,
a panther's on the prowl.

He's turned rogue,
cannot find his mate.

Crouching by the Yamuna,
he guards all its entry points from Gopa

and pounces on maidens
on their way to the river

dragging them to his lair
with a child's ardour.

The women bewitched
by his beauty,

his shining claws and gleaming teeth,
find their hearts torn to shreds.

The beast's hypnotic eyes,
the touch of his scarlet lips,

his tawny pelt,
and forehead marked

with sandal paste,
fuel their desire.

No one knows this panther's origins.
He is none other, says Salabega, than Kanhai.

(Salabega: Prabhanjan Mishra)

The Great Ghost of Pandhari
Pounces upon everyone who passes by.

That forest is haunted by many spirits.
Whoever enters it finds it maddening.

O do not ever go there – you!
Nobody who goes in ever comes back.

Only once did Tuka go to Pandhari:
He hasn't been born ever since.

(Tukaram: Dilip Chitre)

'IS THERE SOME WAY I CAN
REACH YOU?'

Longing

Is there some way I can reach you?
You have no end and no beginning.

I want to praise your good qualities,
but you have no qualities.
I try to think of you in my mind.
You sit behind every thought.

   Is there some way I can reach you?

I want to worship you with my hands,
but you are huge, you fill all space.
I would bring you a gift, but you have everything
in the world.

   Is there some way I can reach you?

I want to see you with my eyes.
You have no visible form.
God on the hill, you're in all these things.
All I can say is, I am yours.

   Is there some way I can reach you?

(Annamacharya: V. Narayana Rao and David Shulman)

Whatever It was

that made this earth
the base,
the world its life,
the wind its pillar,
arranged the lotus and the moon,
and covered it all with folds
of sky

with Itself inside,

to that Mystery
indifferent to differences,

to It I pray,
O Ramanatha.

(Devara Dasimayya: A.K. Ramanujan)

It is the month of Chet,
It is spring. All is seemly –
The humming bumble-bee
And the woodland in flower –
But there is a sorrow in my soul.

The Lord, my Master, is away.
If the Husband comes not home, how can a wife
Find peace of mind?
Sorrows of separation waste away the body.
The koel calls in the mango grove,
Its notes are full of joy.
Why then the sorrow in my soul?
The bumble-bee hovers about the blossoming bough,
O mother of mine, it is like death to me,
For there is a sorrow in my soul.

Nanak says: When the Lord her Master comes home to her,
            Blessed then is the month of Chet.

(Guru Nanak: Khushwant Singh)

She lingers out of doors.
She rushes in
And she rushes out,
Her heart is restless.
Breathing fast,
She gazes at the kadamba wood.
What has happened
That she is not afraid?
The elders chatter
And the wicked gossip.

Is she possessed
By some enchanting god?
Forever restless
Careless of clothes,
Startled, she jumps in her dreams...

Her desire inflamed
By passion and longing,
She reaches for the moon.

Chandidas says that she is caught
In the snare of Kaliya, the dark.

(Chandidas: Deben Bhattacharya)

I don't call you "father" or "mother,"
"O Lord," is good enough for me.
Yet Lord, you won't consider me one of your creatures,
won't show me even a little of your grace.
Alas, if he waits too long to bless his devotees,
do I have no Master
other than the Lord who lives
in Paccilacciramam where wild geese swim in the lakes?

(Sundarar: Indira Viswanathan Peterson)

We're told you're the holiest of holies.
How is it your bhaktas still suffer?
Your bhaktas, you say, are part of your body.
Now who's to blame? The body or its parts?
Shame on the lion, if the bear steals his cub.
Kanhopatra offers up her body, says: Now keep your word.

(Kanhopatra: Jerry Pinto and Neela Bhagwat)

All around us, clouds burst.
Yet with every drop, sister,
this parched body aches
and craves for Krishna.

(Rahim: Mustansir Dalvi)

Don't make me hear all day
    'Whose man, whose man, whose man is this?'

Let me hear, 'This man is mine, mine
    this man is mine.'

O lord of the meeting rivers,
    make me feel I'm a son
    of the house.

(Basavanna: A.K. Ramanujan)

Eating God

The spotless being depicted holding a silver
conch in his left hand will not show his form

to me. He arrives through an underground
spring to liquefy my house's foundations,

to seep into the walls and overflow my heart:
pure torture. Warbling kohl-bird drunk on

honey from the twitching stamen of magnolia
blossoms, intercede to the lord of Venkata

on my behalf, murmur, get him to come.

(Andal: Ravi Shankar)

14

'WHY DON'T YOU SHOW ME YOUR FACE?'

Entreaty

drunken clouds
bring
no message
from my love

frogs
peacocks
fever-birds
chatter
the cuckoo
sings

lightning flashes
in the dark
scared
I want him

the wind is
cool and musical
the clouds
are pouring rain

where are you
Hari

your absence
is venom
in my veins

(Mirabai: Rahul Soni)

You are the forest

you are all the great trees
    in the forest

you are bird and beast
    playing in and out
    of all the trees

O lord white as jasmine
filling and filled by all

why don't you
show me your face?

                        (Akka Mahadevi: A.K. Ramanujan)

Like an elephant
lost from its herd
suddenly captured,

remembering his mountains,
    his Vindhyas,
        I remember.

A parrot
come into a cage
remembering his mate,
        I remember.

O lord white as jasmine
show me
your ways.
    Call me: Child, come here,
        come this way.

                    (Akka Mahadevi: A.K. Ramanujan)

He left me saying he would be back tomorrow.
I've covered the floor of my home
Writing: Tomorrow.
When dawn came, they all enquired:
Tell us, friend,
When will your tomorrow come?
Tomorrow, tomorrow, I gave up my hopes,
My beloved never returned.

Says Vidyapati, listen, beautiful one,
Other women held him back.

(Vidyapati: Deben Bhattacharya)

You dwell in heaven
>stand on the sacred mountain
>sleep on the ocean
>roll around in the earth

yet hidden everywhere
>you grow
>invisibly:

moving within
>numberless outer worlds

playing within my heart
>yet not showing your body

will you always play hide and seek?

(Nammalvar: A.K. Ramanujan)

My bones are immaterial, the lance of my eyes
is unsheathed, insomniac, sunken in sorrow

even when I whirl round like arms of galaxies.
Still I do not see the boat called Vaikunta.

Dear kohl, you know well the pangs of parting
from your beloved, please go to the golden-

hued, Garuda-cloaked lord and convince him
to come to me. I long to bathe his long feet,

the dark lord of Villiputtur, where swans bob,
where my eyes, which have like fighting carp

known no rest, can finally settle. I'm begging.

(Andal: Ravi Shankar)

How much more must I plead, Lord?
How much more jealousy must I bear?
The love of others touches you.
Why do you refuse mine?
I feel no fear of you now.
Not of you, nor of any other.
How much more must I say, Lord?
I don't care if you bear a grudge.
Soyara says: I'm here. I won't budge.

(Soyarabai: Jerry Pinto and Neela Bhagwat)

'I CANNOT FATHOM YOUR LOVE
OF FORM'

Wonder

The flute has but to touch his lips and see –

Women run wild at the sound, out into the forest,
Forgetting to take their garments with them –

The flute has but to touch his lips.

A cow looks up from her grazing,
Her calf lets go of her nipples,

The flute has but to touch his lips,

And a bird shuts his eyes to listen,
Quiet as a seer in deepest contemplation.

Neither creeper nor grass quiver now,
Though a light scented breeze blows between them;

Now even the Jamuna, Surdas, wants to slow down,
Stay back and listen. See: Her waters retreat.

The flute has but to touch his lips.

(Surdas: Anand Thakore)

The Greatness of Pandharpur

No wear! No tear! It's priceless! It's free!
We have seen on the bank of the river Bheema
That which lies beyond all contemplation:
Absolute Being! – with our own eyes!

The inexpressible sprouting out in a form
Leaving out no detail
Without doubt, devotion dispels
All illusion – moving or still!

The frontierless universe
With nothing left beyond itself
Is present here
On the Brick.

Nivrutti marvels
How Pundalik made tangible
As a fully realized form
That which is beyond expression!

(Nivruttinath: Dilip Chitre)

Who is the one
That conceives?
Who is the one
That is born?
O Benevolent One
I cannot fathom
Your love of form

Who is the one
That asks?
Who is the one
That gives?
O Benevolent One
I cannot fathom
Your love of form.

Who is the one
That experiences?
Who creates
That experience?
O Benevolent One
I cannot fathom
Your love of form.

Who is the one
That manifests?
Who is the unmanifested One?
O Benevolent One
I cannot fathom
Your love of form.

Says Tuka, it is
You everywhere
And You are everything
Other than You.

(Tukaram: Dilip Chitre)

Before I could say,

> "He became cowherd
>   fish
>   wild boar,"

he became a million million.

(Nammalvar: A.K. Ramanujan)

The Paradigm

We here and that man, this man,
    and that other in-between,
and that woman, this woman,
    and that other, whoever,

those people, and these,
    and these others in-between,
this thing, that thing,
    and this other in-between, whichever,

all things dying, these things,
    those things, those others in-between,
good things, bad things,
    things that were, that will be,

being all of them,
he stands there.

(Nammalvar: A.K. Ramanujan)

'A MARVEL OF CONTRADICTIONS'

Praise

He cannot be proved, for He is uncreated;
He is without matter, self-existent.
They that serve shall honoured be,
O Nanak, the Lord is most excellent.

Praise the Lord, hear them that do Him praise.
In your hearts His name be graven,
Sorrows from your soul erase
And make your hearts a joyous haven.

The Guru's word has the sage's wisdom,
The Guru's word is full of learning,
For though it be the Guru's word
God Himself speaks therein.

Thus run the words of the Guru:
'God is the destroyer, preserver and creator,
God is the Goddess too.
Words to describe are hard to find,
I would venture if I knew.'
This alone my teacher taught,
There is but one Lord of all creation,
Forget Him not.

(Guru Nanak: Khushwant Singh)

Were I given a hundred thousand tongues instead of one
And the hundred thousand multiplied twenty-fold,
A hundred thousand times would I say, and say again,
The Lord of all the worlds is One.
That is the path that leads
These the steps that mount,
Ascend thus to the Lord's mansion
And with Him be joined in unison.
The sound of the songs of Heaven thrills
The like of us who crawl, but desire to fly.
O Nanak, His grace alone it is that fulfills,
The rest mere prattle, and a lie.

(Guru Nanak: Khushwant Singh)

Simple parrot
imprisoned in your cage,
come here, I will give you
milk and honey to drink,
as much as you wish,
if you will speak for me just once
the sweet name of the Lord who wears the bright young

moon,

king of Tonipuram by the sea,
where the beach is strewn
with clustered coral and pearls!

(Sambandar: Indira Viswanathan Peterson)

Origin of rapture
   Wellspring
   of wisdom
Ambrosial, abundant
   Rim
of the rimless horizon
   Terminus
of the four Vedas –

   your feet,
Mother Abhirami

that crown the head
   of the Lord
   who whirls
through swirling forests
   of white ash.

   Your feet.

(Abhirami Bhattar: Arundhathi Subramaniam)

He used the golden bow
of Mount Meru
    to decimate
    three great cities

and he slayed the elephant
    despatched to annihilate the world,

    then donned its hide
as his mantle.

But you
    you scarred
this warrior's body

with your breasts,

great Goddess,
    you whose golden hands
wielding a bow of sugarcane
and flower-tipped arrows

    are lodged
    forever
    in my heart.

(Abhirami Bhattar: Arundhathi Subramaniam)

The Lord at Play

1

Worker of miracles
    magical dwarf,
       and killer of the demon
         named Honey,

only you can tell us:

becoming fire, water, earth,
    sky, and wind,

becoming father, mother,
    and all the children too
    and all others
    and all things unnamed,

the way you stand there,
being yourself—

what's it all about?

2

O lord unending
    wearing honey flowers
    and basil leaf
    in your hair

tell us this:

as moon
    as sun
        as the amazing numberless stars

as darkness
    and as torrents of rain

as honor
    as shame

and as death
    with his cruel eyes

how fantastic
    can you get?

3

You do stunts
    with your chariots

the discus your weapon:

tell us how

    managing every one of the four ages
    becoming every little thing in them

    harmonious now
        now quite contrary

you stand there

a marvel
    of contradictions!

(Nammalvar: A.K. Ramanujan)

'LIKE A FROG CAUGHT IN THE SNAKE'S MOUTH'

Fear

O Master, come to me,
I waste and will die.
If the Master wills,
I shall meet Him.
If He wills not,
I am lost utterly.
I took the path of falsehood,
And the Master forsook me,
Age has greyed my locks
I have lived many winters
The fires of hell still lie ahead,
And I am afraid.

The bough remains ever green
For the sap that moves within
Night and day, renews life.
If the Name of the Lord courses in your veins,
Life and hope will for ever be green.
Meditate calmly on the Name.
That which ripens slowly ripens best.

Nanak says: Come now, my Love
    Even the Guru pleads for me.

(Guru Nanak: Khushwant Singh)

Tiruvaiyaru is the place
where the female ape, in fright,
leaps up on a branch to look for rainclouds,
taking for thunder the roll of drums
when women dance, going around the shrine
where the Lord dwells who delivers us from fear
when the five senses wander out of their cages,
and cease to function,
the phlegm rises, the reason fails,
and we are afraid.

(Sambandar: Indira Viswanathan Peterson)

In vain I pampered the body's cage,
nurturing evil in my heart.
Like a spoon without a handle,
I can't dip into the ambrosia I seek.
As I think desperate thoughts,
like a frog caught in the snake's mouth,
protect and save me,
O king of Orriyur!

(Appar: Indira Viswanathan Peterson)

How the rain falls
In deadly darkness!
O gentle girl, the rain
Pours on your path
And roaming spirits straddle the wet night.
She is afraid
Of loving for the first time.
O Madhava,
Cover her with sweetness.

How will she cross the fearful river
In her path?
Enraptured with love,
Beloved Radha is careless of the rest.

Knowing so much,
O shameless one,
How can you be so cold towards her?
Whoever saw
Honey fly to the bee?

(Vidyapati: Deben Bhattacharya)

Restless mind, don't infect the heart with fear.
That virus is not for you.
The Infinite knows what you hunger for.
Ask Him to carry you across.

(Lal Ded: Ranjit Hoskote)

And one day
Death shall arrive

to evict this squatter
from his fragile hut of bones

Then as the spirit
    quivers, buckles,
        collapses,

hurry, Goddess Abhirami –

    you that are the primordial note
    plucked by the strings of the veena
    at the dawn of time

Hurry

    with the soft clink
    of braceleted wrists

Hurry

    with your flock of handmaidens
    of the sky

Hurry

    extend a bejeweled hand
    utter the words I need to hear

    Reassure me, say, 'Do not fear.'

(Abhirami Bhattar: Arundhathi Subramaniam)

I beat on your door
Out of fear.

I wasn't yet born,
I was in the womb,
When a great sadness
Came over me.

It hasn't left me since.
It's with me now
When I'm old and infirm
And time shakes me by the hair.

Time strikes the drum.

I've nowhere to turn,
Says Kabir, let me in.

(Kabir: A.K. Mehrotra)

'THE BODY THE SHRINE'

Body

The man with a body grows hungry
The man with a body tells lies
Do not tease me,
The man with a body
Just once
Take on a body like mine
And see for yourself, O Ramanatha.

(Devara Dasimayya: H.S. Shivaprakash)

People,
male and female,
blush when a cloth covering their shame
comes loose.

When the lord of lives
lives drowned without a face
in the world, how can you be modest?

When all the world is the eye of the lord,
onlooking everywhere, what can you
cover and conceal?

(Akka Mahadevi: A.K. Ramanujan)

Age and decrepitude claim you,
    body and mind askew,
    hope of remedy vanished.
    Your wealth's run low too.

That's
    when you turn to religion,
    when flesh tears
    like mouldy cloth.

Akha says,
    you did not know
    how to worship the Lord.
    But are down on fours now,
    hands to floor!

(Akho: Gieve Patel)

The Dude! Bathed, scrubbed,
    perfumed, tucking in
    eats till he bloats
    stud-size.

Battening on
    each pleasure on earth,
    a germ of maya sits concealed
    in that bulk.

That pampered carcass
    believes maya to be his friend.
    But maya will chew him down
    to his entrails.

(Akho: Gieve Patel)

This body that you're fussing over,
this body that you're dolling up,
this body that you're wearing to the party,
this body will end as ash.

(Lal Ded: Ranjit Hoskote)

The walls are made of water, pillared by air,
    sealed together with the mortar of blood,
A cell of veins and meat and bones
    a cage to hold this poor bird.
Who cares what is yours or mine? –
    for we nest in this tree only briefly.
As high as you can build, as low as you can dig,
    your size will never swell the dimensions of a grave;
Those lovely curls, that turban tied so rakishly –
    they'll soon be turned to ash.
If you've counted on the beauty of your wife and home
    without the name of Ram, you've already lost the game.
And me: even though my birth is mean,
    my ancestry by everyone despised,
I have already trusted in you, King Ram,
    says Ravidas, a tanner of hides.

(Ravidas: John Stratton Hawley and Mark Juergensmeyer)

Death has them in its sights,
Both beggar and king.
Man's life is a dancing shadow,
Amounting to nothing.

But the body's a lake,
The soul a swan,
If the chemical on your tongue,
Says Kabir, is called Rama.

(Kabir: A.K. Mehrotra)

With a whole temple
in this body
where's the need
for another?

No one asked
for two.

O Lord of Caves,
if you are stone,
what am I?

(Allama Prabhu: A.K. Ramanujan)

You say some bodies are untouchable.
Tell me what you say of the soul.
You say defilement is born in the body.
If menstrual blood makes me impure,
Tell me who was not born of that blood.
This blood of mine fertilises the world.
Tell me who has not sprung from this source.
Soyara says: this impurity is the cornerstone of your world.
That's why I praise only Panduranga,
Who lives in every body, pure, impure.

(Soyarabai: Jerry Pinto and Neela Bhagwat)

The rich
will make temples for Siva.
What shall I,
a poor man,
do?

My legs are pillars,
the body the shrine,
the head a cupola
of gold.

Listen, O lord of the meeting rivers,
things standing shall fall,
but the moving ever shall stay.

(Basavanna: A.K. Ramanujan)

'LIKE AN ELEPHANT OUT OF CONTROL'

Mind

They searched and searched, searched some more—
it just kept disappearing.
After all that search, when they couldn't find it,
they gave up and said, 'Beyond.'

(Kabir: Linda Hess and Shukdev Singh)

What if Ram had not chased the deer
and Sita not been abducted by Ravan?
There is nothing to be got out of this, Rahim,
what is to be shall be.

(Rahim: Mustansir Dalvi)

Mind, you never lost this delusion.
No wonder Kali won't even look at you.
You claim to know the three worlds are
But an embodiment of Ma
But who'd guess you do the way you
Embody her in shapes of clay to pray to!
She's the one who adorns the earth with
Such priceless gold and gems
Aren't you ashamed of dressing her up
In such cut-price ornaments?
She's the one who lavishes the earth
With delicious food of every kind
Aren't you ashamed of offering her
Sundried rice and soaked gram?
Don't you know she's the one
Looking after the earth so tender-lovingly?
Then why on earth do you insist on offering her
The sacrificial goat, the buffalo and the ram?
Prasad says, bhakti is nothing but adoration.
Your showy pujas may impress folks
But Ma won't take your bribes!

(Ramprasad Sen: Sampurna Chattarji)

Lord, it's up to you
To discipline my mind.
You live in me.

It's like an elephant out of control.
It goes crazy again and again.
It's like mercury, never contained,
always slipping away.

    You live in me.

It's like a deer in the wilderness.
The more you try to catch it,
the more it runs away.
It's like a wild wind at play.

    You live in me.

Like the ocean, it takes in everything.
You have to look after it, god on the hill.
Tell it to come to you.

    You live in me.

        (Annamacharya: V. Narayana Rao and David Shulman)

Hiralal, you never went to Moti's shop
All you ever bought were brass farthings!
Mind, distracted by all that jazz
You lost what's really rich
The stakes were high
You lost them all
Weep all you like
You'll never heal

You're thinking beforehand
Of what's behind you
Sure
That's how it's meant to be
What rules
Past deeds
The mind's fine
Palate

So you made a profit!
Good for you!
That's such a useful skill.
What a waste
Lalon says
All this coming
And
Going

(Lalon Fakir: Sampurna Chattarji)

Listen carefully,
Neither the Vedas
Nor the Qur'an
Will teach you this:
Put the bit in its mouth,
The saddle on its back,
Your foot in the stirrup,
And ride your wild runaway mind
All the way to heaven.

(Kabir: A.K. Mehrotra)

Seeing is one thing,
looking is another.
If both come together,
that is god.

If you look for an elephant,
he comes as an elephant.
If you look for a tree,
he's a tree.
If you look for a mountain,
he'll be a mountain.
God is what you have in your mind.

If you look for empty space,
he appears as space.
If you look for an ocean,
he'll be an ocean.
If you look for a city,
he will come as a city.
God is what you have in your mind.

If you think of the god on the hill,
married to the goddess,
that's who you'll see.
What you look for
is the god in you.
What you see
is the god out there.
God is what you have in your mind.

(Annamacharya: V. Narayana Rao and David Shulman)

'I'M THE GREATEST EXPERT ON GOD'

Hubris, Forgetfulness, Ego Games

The alley is narrow, Rahim,
not wide enough for two bestride;
if your ego persists, there is no Hari,
where Hari is present, there is no ego.

(Rahim: Mustansir Dalvi)

Why was I born?
I who only cared for my pride,
I who was caught in women's snares,
I who failed to think of my dear kinsman,
my ambrosia, the world's beginning and end,
my Lord whose form bright as the sunset sky
lay buried in my heart?

(Appar: Indira Viswanathan Peterson)

What can I say about my crazy ways?
Just laugh them off.
Take care of me.

You speak through me,
and I'm proud of my eloquence.
You control the whole world,
but I think I'm the king.

> *What can I say?*

You create all these people,
and then I think *I'm* my children's father.
You give whatever you have,
but I'm sure I've earned it all.

> *What can I say?*

You give this world and the other,
and I think I've won them by my prayers.
You're not finished with me yet.
I'm the greatest expert
on God.

> *What can I say?*

(Annamacharya: V. Narayana Rao and David Shulman)

Eating God

To dam a flood,
to blow out a forest fire,
to walk on air,
to milk a wooden cow:
any con artist could do it.

(Lal Ded: Ranjit Hoskote)

It's just a clay puppet, but how it can dance!
It looks here, looks there, listens and talks,
    races off this way and that;
it comes on something and it swells with pride,
    but if fortune fades it starts to cry.
It gets tangled in its lusts, in tastes
    of mind, word, and deed,
    and then it meets its end and takes some other form.
Brother, says Ravidas, the world's a game, a magic show,
    and I'm in love with the gamester,
    the magician who makes it go.

(Ravidas: John Stratton Hawley and Mark Juergensmeyer)

Some think of name and honour all the while
And lose all shame in squabbling over these.
Some dwell in ego, with ego compete:
Unwell their minds, diseased with vanity.
Some are so sunk in pretty woman's wiles,
They dance like monkeys to her every whim.
Some find the grandness of kings' courts a lure
And walk with banners tied around their heads.
Some go all day from fire to holy fire,
Engaged to pray to earn a daily wage.
Some prize their wealth above all other things,
Their wives and parents lack enough to eat.
The wives of some, married with due ritual,
Can never come even into their dreams.
Some find their conduct criticised by saints
But blind to advice, brand them enemies.
Some speak of saints, whom they should venerate,
With taunts and taints, their egos to inflate.
Some solipsists, missing the vital spark,
Will still insist the world stands on their work.
Some brahmins, filled to bursting with their rank,
Think Brahma himself not up to their mark.
Some of high caste, greedy for wealth and fame,
Perform the sacred rites only in name.

(Puntanam Namboodiri: Vijay Nambisan)

Lord!
A fire is raging
without fuel.
No one can put it out.
I know it spreads from you, enflaming
the whole world.
Even in water
the flames sprout.
Not one but nine streams
are burning. No one
knows any device.
As the city blazes, the watchman
sleeps happily, thinking,
"My house is secure.
Let the town burn, as long as my things
are saved."
Ram, how your colours flicker!
In a hunchback's arms can a man's desires
be fulfilled?
Even as you think of this, you disappear
from birth to birth, your body forever
unsatisfied. No one is so stupid
as one who knows this
and pretends he doesn't.
Kabir asks, what's the way out
for such a fool?

(Kabir: Linda Hess and Shukdev Singh)

Mind, you don't know the gag
That'll snag the moon
You're all flash
The dance is all
You'd like to grab
The sky
With one big leap

Who gets to the core
Of life's little truths
He who truly relishes
The rasa of love
Go figure
What that love is like
Let your soul awake
To such a coming
Together

You're a fan
You decide
The Deliverer
Will hinder
You
That's the only way
Your love will turn
To worship

Or else
You'll die
A useless death
Bailing out
Water with a thimble

The Deliverer
Is in
The azaan
Of your eyes
Devotee
Here's the ladder
Of here and now
Say *Guru Guru*
Get a grip on it
And climb
Let go
And
You'll slip
Through the gaps
Lalon

(Lalon Fakir: Sampurna Chattarji)

'YOUR HAIR-SPLITTING'S SO MUCH BULLSHIT'

Shedding Cargo, Cutting the Crap

O pundit, your hair-splitting's
So much bullshit. I'm surprised
You still get away with it.

If parroting the name
Of Rama brought salvation,
Then saying *sugarcane*
Should sweeten the mouth,
Saying *fire* burn the feet,
Saying *water* slake thirst,
And saying *food*
Would be as good as a belch

If saying *money* made everyone rich,
There'd be no beggars in the streets.

My back is turned on the world,
You hear me singing of Rama and you smile.
One day, Kabir says,
All bundled up,
You'll be delivered to Deathville.

(Kabir: A.K. Mehrotra)

Turban tilted rakishly
    to hide the bald spot,
    but how will that mask
    the godlessness in your heart?

Such dandy twirled whiskers!
    Such fancy tripping speech!
    Fool! Death tomorrow
    thumps on a slackened drum.

Your charade goes poof,
    a miserable fart.
    Akha says: Rotted doors
    fall apart.

(Akho: Gieve Patel)

Where the creature is
    there is the Creator,
    but you wander elsewhere,
    search in faraway places.

The first false step, says Akha,
    was that you forgot
    to look within.

So you forgot.
    Go then, study
    with a saint. What's gained
    by shows of piety:
    one day all whiskers and beard,
    the next day tonsured, sheared?

(Akho: Gieve Patel)

You speak of caste? Whatever his birth affirms,
Lowborn, or brahmin as his books confirm,
Unless that he be born without a tongue,
Or else by evil chances rendered dumb –
Of all the countless names which praise the Lord,
If daily he says one, just that one word –
Says it when sitting at his tranquil ease,
Or says it in a dream of passing peace,
Or says it lightly, in some mirthful pause,
Or says it rightly, in another's cause,
Says it but once, utters it with his speech –
Wherever he be, the Lord is in his reach.

Why even that? If some day, at some hour
The brave accents fall gently on his ears –
At that moment his human fate bears fruit,
At that moment he gains the Absolute.

(Puntanam Namboodiri: Vijay Nambisan)

They plunge
wherever they see water.

They circumambulate
every tree they see.

How can they know you
O lord
who adore
waters that run dry
trees that wither?

(Basavanna: A.K. Ramanujan)

He is my Master
through whom the light of the Lord manifests itself,
I am his servant
who recites His Name and cherishes His image in my heart.

The pandita parrots scriptures,
but the bhakta realizes its essence,
just as water floats the lotus,
but the black-bee sucks its honey.
Where there is devotion, there is salvation:
the bhakta alone knows this truth,
as it is only the jeweler who
knows the philosopher's stone and speaks of its properties

So Sankara, the servant of Krishna, says:
Offer thy love at the Feet of Govinda,
for he alone is a pandita, he alone is esteemed,
who sings the praises of Hari.

(Sankardeva: based on renderings by B.K. Barua and
Maheswar Neog)

71

Up, woman! Go make your offering.
Take wine, meat and a cake fit for the gods.
If you know the password to the Supreme Place,
you can reach wisdom by breaking the rules.

(Lal Ded: Ranjit Hoskote)

Some, who have closed their eyes, are wide awake.
Some, who look out at the world, are fast asleep.
Some who bathe in sacred pools remain dirty.
Some are at home in the world but keep their hands clean.

(Lal Ded: Ranjit Hoskote)

Numerous worlds there be in regions beyond the skies and
below,
But the research-weary scholars say, we do not know.
The Hindu and the Muslim books are full of theories; the
answer is but one.
If it could have been writ, it would have been, but the
writer thereof be none.
O Nanak, say but this, the Lord is great, in His knowledge
He is alone.

(Guru Nanak: Khushwant Singh)

Why chant the Veda? Why perform sacrifices?
Why study the Lawbooks every day,
why know the six Vedanga texts?
All this is in vain,
if you do not love the Lord.

(Appar: Indira Viswanathan Peterson)

Why rise at dawn and bathe?
Why practice each rite according to the rules?
Why perform sacrifices at great altars of fire?
All this is in vain if you do not say,
"He is my friend."

(Appar: Indira Viswanathan Peterson)

At the Foot of the Mountain

At the foot of the mountain is Damodar Pond.
Mehtaji goes there for his bath and ablutions.
The Dheds,[1] lost in their Hari worship,
bow and offer him their salutations.

At the foot of the mountain is Damodar Pond

Folding their hands in reverence they ask
'Great One, perform a kirtan in our yard.
Your chants will grant us the gift of love supreme
and rid us of the coils of births and deaths.'

At the foot of the mountain is Damodar Pond

A kind Vaishnava that he is, he is touched;
Seeing their folded palms, his compassion flames:
God cannot be where there's inequality,
for Him all human beings are the same.

At the foot of the mountain is Damodar Pond.

'Cleanse the tulsi area with cow urine,' he says,
comes to the village carrying temple oblations at night.
Conch and mridang accompany his prayers;
he leaves still singing his hymns at first light.

At the foot of the mountain is Damodar Pond.

---

[1] *Dheds*: sweepers and cleaners of the untouchable caste

The Nagars[1] rail at him, clap and laugh.
'Are these a Brahmin's ways?' they scoff.
He holds on to his silence, thinking, what answer
can I give these people—shallow and rough.

At the foot of the mountain is Damodar Pond.

'What Brahmin are you, Mehtaji?' they ask.
'You don't know the split between caste and clan?
You stray from our ways and thought, time-worn.'
Says Narasaiyo, folding his hands

'I place my faith in God alone.'
At the foot of the mountain is Damodar Pond.

(Narsinh Mehta: Keki Daruwalla and Meena Desai)

---

[1]*Nagars*: members of the Brahmin community

Pandit, do some research
and let me know
how to destroy transiency.
Money, religion, pleasure, salvation –
which way do they stay, brother?
North, South, East or West?
In heaven or the underworld?
If Gopal is everywhere, where is hell?

Heaven and hell are for the ignorant,
not for those who know Hari.
The fearful things that everyone fears,
I don't fear.
I'm not confused about sin and purity,
heaven and hell.
Kabir says, seekers, listen:
Wherever you are
is the entry point.

(Kabir: Linda Hess and Shukdev Singh)

'DON'T GIVE US YOUR NOWS
AND THENS'

Urgency

What's to come tomorrow
let it come today.
What's to come today
let it come right now.

Lord white as jasmine,
don't give us your *nows* and *thens*!

(Akka Mahadevi: A.K. Ramanujan)

Rana
this shame is
so sweet

condemn or
commend me
I'll carry on

there's no
turning back
on this
one-way street

hermits
speak wisely
sinners
vilify

but Girdhar's
my master
the sinners
can go die

(Mirabai: Rahul Soni)

This songbird craves
but for a glimpse of you.
Come, Sudhakar my love,
wring me dry.

(Rahim: Mustansir Dalvi)

Water soon drains away
from a fish caught in a net.
Observe, Rahim, its pangs of love,
as it chooses death over separation.

(Rahim: Mustansir Dalvi)

Yes, you can stand around
When the oven is burning
But where can you flee
When the whole earth is burning?
When the bank drinks up the water
And the fence grazes the field,
And the housewife steals from her own house,
And the mother's poisoned breast milk kills,
O Kudalasangamadeva
To whom shall I complain?

(Basavanna: H.S. Shivaprakash)

With white hoops on moist mud
with moonlit sand I worship You

and Your brother: You two who stroke ardor's ache.
You, burnt bodiless, save my body as I char

for his sooty resplendence: send me
to him who grasps the sphere spitting fire –

I'll follow him
as liquid shadow.

invisible god of love
with white on wet umber
with rings of serene shimmer

I encircle you with prayer
as my body blazes:
fire me

at him who's cosmic flame
scorch desire: douse
me in his pouring grace

(Andal: Priya Sarukkai Chabria)

I lie here yearning for the familiar sight
of Kannan, my dark lord.
Do not just stand there, mocking me
It is like pouring sour juice upon a raw and open wound.
Instead, bring the golden silk
wrapped around the waist of my great lord
who does not know
the agony of a woman's heart.
Fan me with it and cool my burning fever.

(Andal: Archana Venkatesan)

I cannot bear the day; I cannot bear the night.
I am so much ashamed that I cannot even admit it.

I waste my words like the wind; you do not even taste them.
Your indifference humiliates me; I seethe with rage.

My mind cries to itself;
It chokes, and then it is spent.

Says Tuka, after all, You are omniscient!
How can I argue my hopeless case?

(Tukaram: Dilip Chitre)

Tell me, O God, why you and I
Are cast in the roles of enemy?
Why must you always reveal to me
Only mountainous burdens of suffering?

You give me into that all-consuming hand of time,
Without an iota of liberty.
Muzzled and tied up. Why?
What made you think of this design?

Lord, we placed all our hope in you.
Now we know better!
Hrishikesha, it's you
Who makes us suffer.

Says Nama,
O Lord!
Either have pity on me
Or kill me now.

(Namdev: Dilip Chitre)

I throw ashes at all laws
Made by man or god.
I am born alone,
With no companion.
What is the worth
Of your vile laws
That failed me
In love,
And left me with a fool,
A dumbskull?

My wretched fate
Is so designed
That he is absent
For whom I long.
I will set fire to this house
And go away.

(Chandidas: Deben Bhattacharya)

While you're busy perfuming
Your body with sandalwood,
Someone else is chopping
the wood for your funeral.

A kite string in your hand,
Paan dribbling from your mouth,
You forget that when you die
They'll truss you up with rope,

Just like a common thief,
And put you on the pyre
To burn. Can't you see that
Rama is the only truth, says Kabir,

Everything else a monstrous lie?

(Kabir: A.K. Mehrotra)

Death is standing on your head.
Wake up, friend!
With your house in the middle of traffic,
how can you sleep so sound?

(Kabir: Linda Hess and Shukdev Singh)

'THE WHOLE TRANSACTION IS A FRAUD'

Reproach

The whole transaction is a fraud.
I will have nothing more to do with you.

You do not operate under one name.
You have thousands of aliases.

When one tries to seek your true identity,
You begin to play hide and seek.

Says Tuka,
You are full of mischief.

(Tukaram: Dilip Chitre)

Finally, I have found out your true character, O Lord!
You trick me into serving you.

Mind you, though, my difficulties are only
A burden for you and all these saints:

For you made me eloquent only to praise yourself
Now come out with some real proof.

Look! I am a grocer by profession.
You can't cheat me at a bargain.

Says Tuka, how do you expect me to dance in ecstasy
Before experiencing you?

(Tukaram: Dilip Chitre)

Well Rahim, what was Hari thinking,
stretching my heartstring to the full?
He pulled me taut towards him first,
then wantonly let go.

(Rahim: Mustansir Dalvi)

If we're still strangers
To each other, who's

To blame? Did I
Blunder or did you

Never know
What a heart desired?

One could go on.
Enough, my lord.

Invite me over, says Kabir,
Or come over yourself.

(Kabir: A.K. Mehrotra)

I fritter my life away in lies,
I'm neither a temple servant nor your devotee.
You have not possessed me with your truth,
Nor given me hope for the future state.
Even if I were your servant,
You would ask nothing of me, give nothing,
Say nothing to me!
Yet, are you not my Master from former lives,
O Lord who lives in Onakantanrali?

(Sundarar: Indira Viswanathan Peterson)

I became your slave
even though I couldn't see you,
and now your image still eludes my eyes –
    when people ask me,
    'how does your lord appear?'
    what can I say?

which among all these forms is yours?

(Karaikkal Ammaiyar: Norman Cutler)

friend
I went
and bought
Govind

in secret
you say

I say
boldly
in plain sight

I paid
too much
you say

I say
I weighed
and paid
just right

I gave
my body
my life
my every
precious thing

now show yourself

you promised me
in another life

(Mirabai: Rahul Soni)

'WHO AM I? WHO ARE YOU?'

Doubt, Bewilderment

Lord! I've never known who I really am, or You.
I threw my love away on this lousy carcass
and never figured it out: You're me, I'm You.
All I ever did was doubt: Who am I? Who are You?

(Lal Ded: Ranjit Hoskote)

Grasp the root: something happens.
Don't be lost
in confusion.
Mind-ocean, mind-born waves—
don't let the tide
sweep you away.

(Kabir: Linda Hess and Shukdev Singh)

She's found him, she has, but Radha disbelieves
That it's true, what she sees when her eyes behold
   her master's moonlike face.
Her gaze is fixed, but her mind is glazed;
   her eyes refuse to close;
And her intellect wages a raging debate:
   Is it a dream? Or is this her true Lord?
Her eyes fill and fill with beauty's high pleasure,
   then hide it away in her breast:
Like bees driven wild by any distance from honey
   they dart back and forth from the hoard to the source.
Sometimes she musters her thoughts; she wonders:
   "Who does he love? Who can this Hari be?"
For love, says Sur, is an awkward thing.
   It ripples the mind with waves

(Surdas: John Stratton Hawley and Mark Juergensmeyer)

Tell her he's standing right next to her,
and he's amazed she doesn't see him.

She's thinking so much, and missing him,
that when he comes to her door and calls her,
she doesn't hear.
Right from the beginning, this separation
has worn her down.
Now if anyone tells her the truth,
she doesn't believe him.

> *He's standing right next to her.*

Drowning in sighs, her hair unkempt,
she doesn't know him even when he touches her.
She's been waiting too long. She's so tired.
When he comes for real, she says it's a lie.

> *He's standing right next to her.*

She lies on a bed of flowers,
her sari slipping from her breasts.
He lies down beside her, she doesn't see him.
Then he looks up and makes love to her,
and she says she's had the strangest dream.

He's standing right next to her.

(Annamacharya: V. Narayana Rao and David Shulman)

'I'LL TEAR OFF YOUR WINGS'

Love's Lunacy

I dance
wearing
ankle-bells

people say
I'm mad
mother-in-law says
the ruin
of our clan

Rana
sent me poison
I drank it
and laughed

offered
body and soul
for one look
at you

Girdhar
my master
now let me come
to you

(Mirabai: Rahul Soni)

fever-bird
stop crying
piya-piya

or
I'll tear off
your wings
cut off
your beak
rub salt
in your wounds

I'm aching
for my piya, my lover
I'm his
and he's mine
why should you
call to him

but
if your call
brings him to me
I'll gild
your beak
I'll crown you
king

crow
go tell my lover

his woman
can't eat
without him
she keeps
crying
piya-piya

come back soon
my master

you know all
don't you know
I can't live
without you

(Mirabai: Rahul Soni)

Ma, who can comprehend your compassion
All is madness thanks to your maya, mad girl
No one recognizes anyone in this world of illusion
You know those pretend-Kalis, they do exactly as they see
Who knows for certain what the mad girl's torments may be
Ramprasad says grace and mercy make all troubles flee

(Ramprasad Sen: Sampurna Chattarji)

Seeing the bright moon
Betray the path,
She bent her face
And cried aloud.
She took mascara from her eyes
And painted Rahu
Eating the moon.
O Madhava,
In a foreign land
Harsh is the heart.
Come back.
I have seen your loved one
Frightened of the god of love.
She calls on Siva
Again and again,
Writhing in the dust,
Offering
Her breasts and hands.
Her body once clutched by your fingers,
She cannot bear the southern breeze.
Gone is her life yet hope teases her
And still she plays
With the fangs of a snake.

(Vidyapati: Deben Bhattacharya)

O madman, with the moon-crowned hair,
God of grace, O Lord,
how can I ever forget you?
You dwell forever in my heart.
In Arutturai, shrine of grace,
in Venneynallur on Pennai's southern bank,
you took me for your own –
how can I deny you now?

(Sundarar: Indira Viswanathan Peterson)

When the snake of separation
Bites the body, mantras
Don't work.
Without Ram you can't live
If you live, you go mad.

(Kabir: Linda Hess and Shukdev Singh)

Their eyes deluged
In ecstasy

Their bodies stippled
With goose flesh

Their intellects stunned
Into imbecility

Like drunken bees,
Incoherent, words vaporizing

On their tongues –
Their madness testimony

To your worship, Great Mother,
Unrivalled by any other.

(Abhirami Bhattar: Arundhathi Subramaniam)

'FEED THEM TO THE KITCHEN FIRES'

Violence, Cannibalism

I hacked my way through six forests
until the moon woke up inside me.
The sky's breath sang through me,
dried up my body's substance.
I roasted my heart in passion's fire
and found Shankara!

(Lal Ded: Ranjit Hoskote)

I pestled my heart in love's mortar,
roasted it and ate it up.
I kept my cool but you can bet I wasn't sure
whether I'd live or die.

(Lal Ded: Ranjit Hoskote)

I melt. I fray. But he does not care
if I live or die.
If that stealthy thief, that duplicitous Govardhana
should even glance at me
I shall pluck these useless breasts of mine
from their roots
I will fling them at his chest
and staunch the fire scorching me.

(Andal: Archana Venkatesan)

I love the Handsome One:
　　he has no death
　　decay nor form
　　no place or side
　　no end nor birthmarks.
　　I love him O mother. Listen.

I love the Beautiful One
　　with no bond nor fear
　　no clan no land
　　no landmarks
　　for his beauty.

So my lord, white as jasmine, is my husband.

Take these husbands who die,
　　decay, and feed them
　　to your kitchen fires!

(Akka Mahadevi: A.K. Ramanujan)

Cripple me, father,
that I may not go here and there.
Blind me, father,
that I may not look at this and that.
Deafen me, father,
that I may not hear anything else.

Keep me
at your men's feet
looking for nothing else,
O lord of the meeting rivers

(Basavanna: A.K. Ramanujan)

Chewing slowly,
Only after I'd eaten
My grandmother,
Mother,
Son-in-law,
Two brothers-in-law,
And father-in-law
(His big family included)
In that order,
And had for dessert
The town's inhabitants,

Did I find, says Kabir,
The beloved that I've become
One with.

(Kabir: A.K. Mehrotra)

My Lord, My Cannibal

1

My dark one
   stands there as if nothing's
      changed
after taking entire
into his maw
   all three worlds
      the gods
   and the gods
   who hold their lands
   as a mother would
      a child in her womb—

and I
   by his leave
have taken him entire

and I have in my belly
for keeps.

3

While I was waiting eagerly for him
    saying to myself,

    "If I see you anywhere
        I'll gather you
           and eat you up,"

he beat me to it
    and devoured me entire,

    my lord dark as raincloud,
        my lord self-seeking and unfair.

                  (Nammalvar: A.K. Ramanujan)

The Takeover

1

Poets,
   beware, your life is in danger:

the lord of gardens is a thief,
      a cheat,
   master of illusions;

he came to me,
      a wizard with words,
   sneaked into my body,
      my breath,

with bystanders looking on
      but seeing nothing,
   he consumed me
      life and limb,

and filled me,
      made me over
   into himself.

4

My lord
    who lives in the city
    of names
came here today

said he'd never leave
    entered me
        filled my heart

I've caught him
    the big-bellied one
        not content yet
    with all that guzzling
        on the sevenfold clouds
        the seven seas
        the seven mountains
        and the world that holds them all

I've caught him
    I contain him now

(Nammalvar: A.K. Ramanujan)

'TAKE ME'

God as Lover

To the Foot of the Bed

To the foot of the bed I'll fasten your arms
with flower-ropes shamelessly.
Who will free you from the temple of my body?
Rivals? What can they do but flame in anger?

To the foot of the bed I'll fasten your arms.

You are the gardener, I the flowering vine;
Why plant me if you will not water me?
You are the honey bee seduced by my love,
You, dying in the fragrance of my lotus heart.

To the foot of the bed I'll fasten your arms.

Love's essence and lover should be one—
Yours is the divine surrender of body and mind.
Says Narsaiyo: Gopi, won't you teach me
how to burrow into his heart and win?

To the foot of the bed I'll fasten your arms.

(Narsinh Mehta: Keki Daruwalla and Meena Desai)

only Girdhar
is mine
no one else

no one else
I've hunted
the world over

left family
and kin
to sit with
hermits

rejoiced
for the pious
wept
for the world

watered
the tree of love
with
my tears

kept
the essence
discarded
the rest

Rana
sent me poison
I drank it
happily

I am in love

who cares
what happens
next

(Mirabai: Rahul Soni)

Radha is lost to the onslaught of love.
She weeps from tree to tree and finally succumbs,
    searching through the forests and groves.
Her braid—a peacock grasps it, thinking it a snake;
    her lotus feet attract the bees;
The honey of her voice makes the crow in the kadamb tree
    caw, caw to mimic its cuckoo;
Her hands—the tender leaves of blossom-bringing Spring:
    the parrot, when he sees, comes near to taste;
And the full moon in her face inspires the cakor bird
    to drink the water washing from her eyes.
Her despair, her desperation—the Joy of the Yadus sees it
    and appears at her side just in time;
Surdas' Lord takes that seedbud of new birth
    and cradles it, a newborn in his arms.

(Surdas: John Stratton Hawley and Mark Juergensmeyer)

Cool rain clouds, *karuvilai* blossoms,
kaya flowers, lotuses, recurrently urge
me to sup at Hrsikesa's feet, his limbs
sweaty, quivering in time like a veena
string, the universe waiting, watching.
I'd give him the food he most desired.
Just leave me alone with him.

(Andal: Ravi Shankar)

It's ages since I last saw you, dear.
Just as well I'm alive, or I wouldn't be here
To see you. But I *am* alive,
And so we've got to see each other:
Or it would have been out of the question.

I bore so much, being of the sex that's weaker.
A stone under the same duress would have fractured.

Time – for an unfortunate – passes slowly.
I presume you, in Mathura, must have been okay?

I don't think of my pain except momentarily,
Your happiness is my happiness, necessarily.

It seems like today all my sorrows are over.
The treasure that went missing has been recovered.

Now let the cuckoos arrive and make music.
Let there be coloratura in the bees' buzzing.

Let the southern breeze blow more slowly.
And let the moon ascend in the sky.

Inspired by the goddess, Chandidas says:
There can be no sorrow after such togetherness.

(Chandidas: Amit Chaudhuri)

I have Maya for mother-in-law;
    the world for father-in-law;
    three brothers-in-law, like tigers;

    and the husband's thoughts
    are full of laughing women;
        no god, this man.

And I cannot cross the sister-in-law.

But I will
give this wench the slip
and go cuckold my husband with Hara, my Lord.

    My mind is my maid:
    by her kindness, I join
    my Lord
        my utterly beautiful Lord
        from the mountain-peaks,
        my lord white as jasmine,
and I will make Him
my good husband.

                (Akka Mahadevi: A.K. Ramanujan)

She whose heart is full of love
Is ever in bloom.
Joy is hers for she has no love of self.
Only those who love You
Conquer love of self.
Come, Lord, and abide in me.

Many a garment did I wear,
The Master willed not and
His palace was barred to me.
When He wanted me, I went
With garlands and strings of jewels and raiment of finery.

Nanak says: A bride welcomed in the Master's mansion
        Has found her true Love.

(Guru Nanak: Khushwant Singh)

O friend, I cannot tell you
Whether he was near or far, real or a dream.
Like a vine of lightning,
As I chained the dark one,
I felt a river flooding in my heart.
Like a shining moon,
I devoured that liquid face.
I felt stars shooting around me.
The sky fell with my dress,
Leaving my ravished breasts.
I was rocking like the earth.
In my storming breath
I could hear my ankle bells,
Sounding like bees.
Drowned in the last waters of dissolution,
I knew that this was not the end.

Says Vidyapati:
How can I possibly believe such nonsense?

(Vidyapati: Deben Bhattacharya)

Love Poems: The Playboy

1

Don't tell us those lies,

heaven and earth
    know your tricks.

Just one thing,
    my lord of the ancient wheel
        that turns at your slightest wish:

while all those girls
—their words pure honey—
stand there
wilting for love of you,

don't playact here and sweet-talk
    our lisping mynahs,
    our chattering parrots!

3

Pure one,
    you devoured once
        the sea-surrounded world.

Great one,
    it isn't right to grab
        our dolls and toys.

What's wrong is wrong
    even for you.

You tease us with sweet talk:
if my brothers hear of it,

they won't wait to see
    right and wrong,
they'll just bring out
    their sticks

and beat you up.

4

Rich and perfect sound
    of strings
    on an ancient lute

other than all others
    that good men study
purity
    sweetness of sugarcane
       and ambrosia

O dark raincloud
    Krsna

without you
    I'm not:

take me

(Nammalvar: A.K. Ramanujan)

'I WILL NOT UTTER YOUR NAME AGAIN'

Rage

I will not utter your name again.
I will not work as you ask any more.

The more words I use, the more absurd this becomes.
I speak of your attributes and find flaws of my own speech.

Who is going to make all those trips to your house and back
Any more? Certainly not me!

Says Tuka, haven't I got all that I want
Right here with me?

(Tukaram: Dilip Chitre)

I shouldn't speak, but the situation compels me
The whole world goes hoarse appealing to you

O conjuror who has spread out this vast show
I know you are really a beggar worth nothing

Having become your dependents, we have become shameless
And therefore we put up with you

We do not know how you will contrive
To end all this clamour created by us

Says Tuka, you are fair indeed! My Lord,
You accept my service without any response

(Tukaram: Dilip Chitre)

You haven't yet paid me my price, my wages due,
Let us see who wins when it's time to settle our accounts

As for me, I am so desperate, I have staked my whole life,
I wonder if you have such guts

So far, O Hari, you have cheated millions at this game
But I am something else, I won't let you escape

I suffered a lot before I came across you
And learnt your name and identity

That was the mistake I made just once, says Tuka,
Now I am going to square with you

(Tukaram: Dilip Chitre)

Get lost, you dirty flirt
I don't need you any more
You have deceit stamped all over you –
the telltale smears of a woman's kohl
red smudges from her lips
and paint from her feet
tell their own sordid story.

How could you visit her?
Tell me, whose wife,
whose daughter was she?
Your fingers are bereft of their precious rings –
did she loot them to give you her company?
You seem fatigued, your eyes swollen –
didn't she allow you a wink of sleep?
And the lacerations on your skin,
did she scratch you with her bangles
in the course of your fevered lovemaking?

What of my sacrifices, you shameless rogue?
I risked my reputation, suffered indignities
to win your affection.

Salabega says, but wasn't it
your own lack of caution, Radha?
The lady messenger you sent
to your lover last evening,
where is she this morning?

(Salabega: Prabhanjan Mishra)

When I'm done being angry,
then I'll make love.
Right now, you should be glad
I'm listening.

When you flash that big smile,
I smile back. It doesn't mean I'm not angry.
You keep looking at me,
so I look too. It isn't right
to ignore the boss.

>   *Right now you should be glad.*

You say something, and I answer.
That doesn't make it a conversation.
You call me to bed, I don't make a fuss.
But unless I want it myself,
it doesn't count as love.

>   *Right now you should be glad.*

You hug me, I hug you back.
You can see I'm still burning.
I can't help it, god on the hill,
if I'm engulfed in your passion.

>   *Right now you should be glad.*

(Annamacharya: V. Narayana Rao and David Shulman)

Good that we've found out
What makes you Almighty!
Now nobody can keep it
A secret.

Why did you beat me up until now?
Now
You and I
Are equal.

Whatever we call you
Is your quality.
At times, I will even
Curse you.

Shame on you! You have no pedigree!
You are casteless! You are a thief!
You are the son of a whore,
As everyone knows!

Says Nama, I am hopping mad now!
I'll fight with you
With the frenzied mouth
Of a maniac!

(Namdev: Dilip Chitre)

'HE'S MY SLAVE'

The Politics of Intimacy

He's the master. What can I say
when he says I'm better than the others?

I don't even have to ask.
He takes whatever I say as a command.
Why should I brag?
My husband is under my thumb.

   He's the master.

Who am I to serve him, when *he*
takes joy in serving me?
How can I tell you the thousand ways
he's with me?
He knows everything, just like god,
and *he* praises me.

   He's the master.

I'm always in his arms.
He's always laughing with me.
He's the god on the hill
and I'm Alamelumanga.
Do I have to make a statement?
He's my slave.

   He's the master.

(Annamacharya: V. Narayana Rao and David Shulman)

Strange Ecstasy and Joy Unique

Strange ecstasy and joy unique:
the son of Nand conjures a leela
to pleasure his beloved proud,
dons garments and adornments strange.
    Here's ecstasy and joy unique

He oscillates upon the swing,
studded with pearls and gems, the swing.
The Gopis through their half drawn veils,
unseen themselves, gaze at his face.
    What ecstasy and joy unique

Body and limb in saffron paste
anointed; unmatched his attire –
an elephant-pearl drops down his nose,
to wet, impassioned lips;
    What ecstasy and joy unique.

Garbed in yellow silk, with love
He wears a sari splashed with dark,
his ringing anklets dance away
to humour her he wears a bodice.
    Strange is the ecstasy of joy

Red lacquered are her tender feet,
studded with gems the anklet-bands,
bracelet and bangle are of gold,
a black braid swaying down the back;
    Strange ecstasy and joy unique

Floral garlands round the head,
the eyes lined with antimony
Narasaiya's Swami, great to meet you
Who can pen your pure resplendence?
    Strange is this joy and ecstasy.

(Narsinh Mehta: Keki Daruwalla and Meena Desai)

I have let my veil drop to my shoulders.
Bare-headed, I shall walk through the market.
In my hands the cymbals, on my shoulder the veena
Let who will try and stop me now.
Come wish me well, anoint my wrists with oil.
Jani says: I have become your whore, Keshava.
I have come now to wreck your home.

(Janabai: Jerry Pinto and Neela Bhagwat)

The elephant is huge
Can you say, 'The driver's hook is small?'
No Father, you cannot.
The mountain is huge
Can you say, 'The lightning bolt is small?'
No Father, you cannot.
Darkness is immense
Can you say, 'The lamp is small?'
No Father, you cannot.
Forgetfulness is immense
Can you say, 'The heart
that remembers you is small?'
No Father, O Kudalasangamadeva,
You cannot.

(Basavanna: H.S. Shivaprakash)

A Woman to Her Reluctant Lover

Because I'm a good woman, I forgave you this time.
Would any other woman have let you off?

You follow me around like a servant,
you say humble things,
yet when I ask you to come home, you don't.
Why do you hurt me like this?

Now I've got you all alone.
If I hold you prisoner in this house,
who is there to release you?

> *Because I'm a good woman*

You hold my hands, you say nice things.
But when I ask you to get into bed,
you say, 'I've taken a vow,' and do nothing.

Now I've caught you.
If I tie you down to my bed,
who is there to release you?

> *Because I'm a good woman*

Only for a bet in a game you enter my bedroom.
When I call you, 'My handsome,
my Muvva Gopala!' why this indifference, dear parrot
in the hand of the Love God?

If I choose to make love to you now,
Who is there to stop me?

Because I'm a good woman

(Kshetrayya: A.K. Ramanujan, V. Narayana Rao and
David Shulman)

Just calling a large thing small, Rahim,
does not diminish its size.
Krishna, who lifted the vast mount Govardhan
won't take it amiss if called Murlidhar.

(Rahim: Mustansir Dalvi)

'YOU DON'T HAVE THAT SKILL'

Irony, Irreverence

Imagine that I wasn't here. What would you do with your
                                                    kindness?
You get a good name because of me.

I'm number one among idiots. A huge mountain of ego.
Rich in weakness, in giving in to my senses.
You're lucky you found me. Try not to lose me.

   Imagine that I wasn't here.

I'm the Emperor of Confusion, of life and death.
Listed in the book of bad karma.
I wallow in births, womb after womb.
Even if you try, could you find another like me?

   Imagine that I wasn't here.

Think it over. By saving someone so low,
you win praise all over the world.
You get merit from me, and I get life
out of you. We're right for each other,
god on the hill.

   Imagine that I wasn't here.

(Annamacharya: V. Narayana Rao and David Shulman)

Just try getting past me, Ma.
What kind of mother would snatch a banana from her son's
hand, Ma?
I'll hide away in such a hideaway, search high and low you
won't find me, Ma!
Just as a cow goes after her calves, you'll come chasing after
me, Ma.
Prasad says, the only way you can get away with such
eyewash is to find a dummy, Ma.
If you can't get past me, Ma, then Shiv will be your Daddy!

(Ramprasad Sen: Sampurna Chattarji)

In everlasting bondage to you, I became your slave,
spurning all other masters.
With smouldering fire inside me,
pale of face, possessed by you,
when I tell you of my pain,
you say nothing.
May you live long, my Lord!

(Sundarar: Indira Viswanathan Peterson)

I have praised you, saying all I can say,
but I can't get anything out of you.
Onakantanrali's Lord, tell me,
how will you rule us
when you won't give up this wretched life
of wandering all day
with a toothless skull for a begging bowl?

(Sundarar: Indira Viswanathan Peterson)

I, only I, am best at being worst, Lord.
It's me! The others are powerless to match me.
    I set the pace, forging onward, alone.
All those others are a flock of amateurs,
    But I have practiced every day since birth,
And look: you've abandoned me, rescuing the rest!
    How can I cause life's stabbing pain to cease?
You've favoured the vulture, the hunter, tyrant, whore,
    And cast me aside, the most worthless of them all.
Quick, save me, says Sur, I'm dying of shame:
    Who was ever finer at failure than I?

(Surdas: John Stratton Hawley and Mark Juergensmeyer)

We get a lot out of you.
You don't have that skill.
God, your servants are better than you.

We grab you with a show of devotion.
We stick you in our mind.
For a little basil on your feet,
we've got freedom wholesale.
Your servants are very clever.

    You don't have that skill.

Giving back what you've created,
we suck up all your goodness.
We've figured it out.
We bow once and twice, and put the burden
on you.

    You don't have that skill.

We bring water from the pond, sprinkle a little on you,
and get whatever we ask.
God on the hill, with tricks like these,
we always come out on top

    You don't have that skill.

(Annamacharya: V. Narayana Rao and David Shulman)

'WHY WAS I BORN?'

Despair

Like a silkworm weaving
her house with love
from her marrow,
                and dying
in her body's threads
winding tight, round
and round,
            I burn
desiring what the heart desires.

Cut through, O lord,
my heart's greed,
and show me
your way out,

O lord white as jasmine.

(Akka Mahadevi: A.K. Ramanujan)

143

Once, a slave of past karma,
I failed to remember my Lord.
Now, having gone mad,
I babble like a fool.
I cannot hold in my heart
The god who is all the goodness
that dwells in me.
Why was I born?

(Appar: Indira Viswanathan Peterson)

The Ninth Song

An exquisite garland lying on her breasts
Is a burden to the frail wasted girl.
  Krishna, Radhika suffers in your desertion.

Moist sandalbalm smoothed on her body
Feels like dread poison to her.
  Krishna, Radhika suffers in your desertion.

The strong wind of her own sighing
Feels like the burning fire of love.
  Krishna, Radhika suffers in your desertion.

Her eyes shed tears everywhere
Like dew from lotuses with broken stems.
  Krishna, Radhika suffers in your desertion.

Her eyes see a couch of tender shoots,
But she imagines a ritual bed of flames.
    Krishna, Radhika suffers in your desertion.

She presses her palm against her cheek,
Wan as a crescent moon in the evening.
    Krishna, Radhika suffers in your desertion.

'Hari! Hari!' she chants passionately,
As if destined to die through harsh neglect.
    Krishna, Radhika suffers in your desertion.

May singing Jayadeva's song
Give pleasure to the worshipper at Krishna's feet!
    Krishna, Radhika suffers in your desertion.

(Jayadeva: Barbara Stoler Miller)

In the garden the bee lingers;
so many fragrant flowers there.
In the senses the creature lingers;
finally it goes out in despair.

(Kabir: Linda Hess and Shukdev Singh)

Life has stumbled, stumbled, unraveled,
Roped to politics and salary and sons.
    Without my even noticing, my life has ambled off
And gotten tangled in a snare of illusion so foolproof
    That now I cannot break it or loosen its grip.
Songs of the Lord, gatherings of the good –
    I left myself hanging in air without either
Like an overeager acrobat who does just one more trick
    Because he cannot bear to close the show.
What splendor, says Sur, can you find in flaunting wealth
    When your husband, your lover, has gone?

(Surdas: John Stratton Hawley and Mark Juergensmeyer)

What have You done, O Gopala!
What have You done to my mind, O Lord!
All my days pass only in vain.

In the midst of this dense forest
    we move about as deer
    chased by Time's hunter,
    and mauled by dogs of passion and anger.
Helpless without the Lord's kindness,
    how will we get out of this maze
    with hearts laden with fear?
Two tigers – one of greed and the other of desire
    follow wherever we go.
And encircled as we are
    and minds enfeebled,
    we find no freedom from the shackles of gloom.
O Lord! I pray to Your Feet, get us out of this mesh,
Sankara prays for Your Grace.

(Sankaradeva: Amaresh Datta)

She Said:
Some send their heart as a messenger
to do their bidding
thinking 'It's an innocent heart, it's *my* heart.'
They should abandon such notions.
My steadfast heart left to place a message
at the feet of the one
who ripped the broad chest of the golden one
but it abandoned me, wanders even now.

(Nammalvar: Archana Venkatesan)

I'm towing my boat across the ocean with a thread.
Will he hear me and help me across?
Or am I seeping away like water from a half-baked cup?
Wander, my poor soul, you're not going home anytime soon.

(Lal Ded: Ranjit Hoskote)

'GOD IS VISITING YOU'

Derailment

When cinders rain down,
Be like the water.
When in the water deluge,
Be like the wind.
When in the great deluge,
Be like the sky.
When in the cosmic deluge,
Give yourself up,
Become Gogeshwara himself.

(Allama Prabhu: H.S. Shivaprakash)

That which smoulders, burns itself out.
The extinguished can never reignite.
Those in love will blaze again, Rahim
each time you snuff them out.

(Rahim: Mustansir Dalvi)

When I board the boat of the mind
and strike out with the oars of my wit,
when I load the cargo of anger,
and row into the deep sea
when, dashing against the rocks of lust,
the boat capsizes,
then, as my reason fails,
give me the consciousness
that will make me think of you,
O king of Orriyur!

(Appar: Indira Viswanathan Peterson)

What have I gained
Saying Krishna and Krishna.
My heart is bruised raw,
Life simply sizzles
And I am dying of the fire of my mind.
In Gokula, the town of the cowherds,
Nothing is forbidden!
They act as they wish.
The girls full of youth
Are ladies of homes.
Only Radha is the scandalous one!

Since the cruel god that created love
Made it dependent on the other's response
I have no wish to live.
And I beg you not to name a girl Radha again.

(Chandidas: Deben Bhattacharya)

When He comes
Out of the blue
A meteorite
Shattering your home
Be sure
God is visiting you

When a catastrophe
Wipes you out
And nothing remains
But God and you
God is visiting you

When your language
Is stripped naked
Never to be clothed
In falsehood again
Be sure
God is visiting you

When your humanness
Is rent and riven
Never to be pieced
Together again
Be sure
God is visiting you

When you are
Beyond all hope
When you call
Nothing your own
Be sure God is visiting you

When you are robbed
Of the whole world
And your voice
Becomes eloquent
Be sure
God is visiting you.

See how God has
Grabbed the whole of him!
Tuka is raging
Like God Himself!

(Tukaram: Dilip Chitre)

'THE YOGI'S A SOLITARY'

In the World but Not of It

Here is a fine fix, Rahim,
which path should I choose?
This world will not abide my truth,
by my falsehoods I will forsake Ram.

(Rahim: Mustansir Dalvi)

Wisest to play the fool. Lynx-eyed, play blind.
Prick-eared, be deaf.
Polished, lie dull among the dull.
Survive.

(Lal Ded: Ranjit Hoskote)

The yogi's a solitary

He doesn't go on pilgrimages
Or to religious fairs
Or attend congregations
He doesn't keep fasts

He doesn't have a travel bag
Or utensils to cook in
Or a plate to eat from
He doesn't carry a purse
He doesn't rub
His body with ash

He doesn't have an alms bowl
But never goes hungry
At night
After his wanderings
He returns to his house
And sleeps in the courtyard

You can't meet him
Says Kabir
He's left the country
We're citizens of
And he's not coming back

(Kabir: A.K. Mehrotra)

I won't be wheedled if you wheedle me again, my dear.
The fearless Way is my sole aim, won't sway back and forth
in fear, my dear.
Enamoured of worldly goods, won't wallow in venom's
well, my dear.
Taking joy and sorrow as the same, won't rouse my mind's
flame, my dear.
Maddened by the greed for wealth, won't plead from door
to door, my dear.
Touched in the head by hope, won't openly speak my
mind, my dear.
Trapped in illusion's snare, won't hang from love's tree,
my dear.
Ramprasad says, I've drunk milk and won't be watered
down, my dear.

(Ramprasad Sen: Sampurna Chattarji)

The man of the house says he's found a guru.
    Mother Mesai,[1] now what do I do?

I have a family, hungry mouths to feed.
    Namdev, my Lord, pays them no heed.

Mesai, I'm asking you for aid.
    I can't see anyone else who will help.

My husband has Vitthala on his mind.
    And fills the house with others of his kind.

They dance, they sing, they touch each other's feet
    They chant Vitthala's name and joy breaks free.

Poor Gonai,[2] you birthed a white stone
    Even that Vitthala claimed for His own.

Mesai, how would a woman not be vexed?
    Mother, you tell me, what comes next?

              (Rajai: Jerry Pinto and Neela Bhagwat)

---

[1] *Mother Mesai*: a village goddess
[2] *Gonai*: Namdev's mother and Rajai's mother-in-law

159

'THOSE WHO KEEP THE BAD COMPANY OF RAMA'

Contagion, Community

Think twice before you keep
The bad company
Of someone like me.

The bitter neem that keeps
The bad company
Of a sandalwood tree
Begins to smell like sandalwood.

The piece of iron that keeps
The bad company
Of the philosopher's stone
Turns into gold

Waters that drain
Into the Ganges
Become the Ganges.

And those who keep
The bad company
Of Rama, says Kabir,
End up

A bit like Rama.

(Kabir: A.K. Mehrotra)

The regal realm with the sorrowless name:
    they call it Queen City, a place with no pain,
No taxes or cares, none owns property there,
    no wrongdoing, worry, terror, or torture.
Oh my brother, I've come to take it as my own,
    my distant home, where everything is right.
That imperial kingdom is rich and secure,
    where none are third or second – all are one;
Its food and drink are famous, and those who live there
    dwell in satisfaction and in wealth.
They do this or that, they walk where they wish,
    they stroll through fabled palaces unchallenged.
Oh, says Ravidas, a tanner now set free,
    those who walk beside me are my friends.

(Ravidas: John Stratton Hawley and Mark Juergensmeyer)

To the gift of elephants
I will say no
To the gift of a huge fortune
I will say no
To the gift of a vast empire
I will say no
But, to the gift of the wise sayings
Of your devotees,
Just for a moment
I will even give you away
O Ramanatha.

(Devara Dasimayya: H.S. Shivaprakash)

My head? Sold to your feet.
My speech? Only your name.
My eyes? See only you.
My body? Laid out before you.

Vatsara says: Keep company with saints;
Cheat death.

(Vatsara: Jerry Pinto and Neela Bhagwat)

The Name

The name of Rama is a universal tree
That shelters us in these fallen times –

And merely recalling it has taught me
To be true to my own:

For I, Tulsidas, who was as scrawny and dry
As a leaf of cannabis,

Have now turned as green and life-giving,
As a leaf of the tulsi-plant;

The name of Rama has brought me to delight in my own.

(Tulsidas: Anand Thakore)

I Have Wasted Much

I have wasted much but now no more –

The night of my existence has passed;
I have woken and will not unroll my sleeping mat again;

For I have found this jewel, this name of Rama
That is now on my lips; and close to my heart I shall keep
it safe –

I have slept long but now no more.
This dark pure form of Rama, is a touchstone

Against which I shall rub the gold of pure consciousness –
Ha, yes they have laughed at me all night, loud and long –

My eyes and ears, my skin, my nostrils and my tongue –
But now that the lord has brought them into my stride,

They shall laugh no more!
See: my heart has turned into a little honey-bee

Who will find his true place, soon, surely,
At the lotus-feet of the lord.

(Tulsidas: Anand Thakore)

Lord of the forsaken
Stanced on the Brick
Makes his devotees fearless
With his inviting arms

Experience liberation sharing meals together
Men women children all
He gives to each whatever they fancy
Lovingly fondling every face

Says come I'll give you
All the joy I have

Says Chokha He is
So devoted to his devotees
He is really present
Where his name is spoken

(Chokhamela: Dilip Chitre)

And then you drenched me
with your grace,
　　colonized me, claimed me.

Is it fair now to deny the fact?

Even if I plunge headlong
　　into the ocean now
it's your call –

Fish me out
　　or leave me to drown.

You that are One
You that are Many
You that are beyond
　　Form.

Your call, my Uma.

　　　　　　(Abhirami Bhattar: Arundhathi Subramaniam)

'WHATEVER MY HANDS DID WAS
WORSHIP'

The Way

Everyone pierces the hide of cattle
With awareness.
Everyone pierces the hide of cattle
In forgetfulness.
But I pierce the hide
Of dead cattle.
I cut away the hide
And the truthful ones put sandals on
I expect them to show me
Emptiness.
Take your paths, all of you
Mine is the path
Of the master of lust, dust and smoke.
That is enough for me.

(Dhoolaiah, the cobbler: H.S. Shivaprakash)

Here I come, a ferryman without a body
To the great flowing river
If you pay the price—
Your mind
That grasps and lets go,
I shall take you across
The great stream
To the end,
To the village
Without words or limits,
Says Chowdaiah, the ferryman.

(Chowdaiah, the ferryman: H.S. Shivaprakash)

Plow the field with true faith.
Sow the seed of love, water it with patience,
and pull out falsehood's weeds.
Look into yourself,
build a fence with virtue.
Stand rooted in the right path –
Harvest the state of Siva!

(Appar: Indira Viswanathan Peterson)

I've never known how to tan or sew,
   though people come to me for shoes.
I haven't the needle to make the holes
   or even the tool to cut the thread.
Others stitch and know, and tie themselves in knots
   while I, who do not knot, break free.
I keep saying Ram and Ram, says Ravidas,
   and Death keeps his business to himself.

(Ravidas: John Stratton Hawley and Mark Juergensmeyer)

Until you wake up to what you really are
You'll be like the man who searches the whole jungle
    for a jewel that hangs at his throat.
Oil, wick and fire: until they mingle in a cruse
    they scarcely produce any light,
So how can you expect to dissipate the darkness
    simply by talking about lamps?
You're the sort of fool who sees your face
    in a mirror, befouled by inky filth,
And proceeds to try to erase the blackness
    by cleaning the reflection to a shine.
Surdas says, it's only now the mind can see—
    now that so countless many days are lost and gone—
For who has ever recognized the brilliance of the sun
    but by seeing it through eyes gone blind?

(Surdas: John Stratton Hawley and Mark Juergensmeyer)

Your waist slender,
swathed in soft vermilion silk
your breasts heavy
with streaming garlands of pearl
your dark tresses woven
with fragrant jasmine, pursued
by clouds
    of maddened bees.

It's enough
    to sit alone
    and gaze at you
three-eyed Goddess.

Who needs to go meditate?

                   (Abhirami Bhattar: Arundhathi Subramaniam)

The Master Weaver

You haven't puzzled out
any of the Weaver's secrets:
    it took Him
a mere moment
to stretch out the whole universe
    on His loom.

While you were there,
listening
    to the Vedas and Puranas,
I was here,
spreading out
    the threads for my warp.

He fashioned His loom
    out of earth and sky:
He plied the sun and moon
simultaneously
    as his twin shuttles.

When He worked the pair
of treadles in the pit below
    in tandem,
I acknowledged Him
in my mind
    as a master weaver.

I found His signs,
The signs of a weaver,
    inside my house:
in a flash
I recognized Him
    as Rama.

Kabir says, I've smashed
    my loom:
only the Weaver
can mesh
    thread with thread.

(Kabir: Vinay Dharwadker)

Whatever my hands did was worship,
whatever my tongue shaped was prayer.
That was Shiva's secret teaching:
I wore it and it became my skin

(Lal Ded: Ranjit Hoskote)

Whirl around yourself
And the world
Seems to whirl
Around you

Stand still
And everything
Is stilled
Within a vast stillness

Yell
And echoes will ring
Says Tuka –
When clouds race
The moon seems to run

(Tukaram: Dilip Chitre)

'WHAT PROFIT WILL YOU GET?'

God as Taxman, Burglar, Businessman

Advice to an Angry Wife: VI

Pandurang, the noble collector of revenue,
Gives us our share of what we reap.

He asks us to repay seventy per cent
Of what we've owned in the past;
And we've so far cleared only ten per cent.

Sitting on a cot in our living-room,
He points to all our possessions:
The storage bin, the pots and pans, the cattle we own.

If I bargain and argue with Him, He keeps His cool.
He says, "Just pay up all your dues and what you reap
Will be all yours."

Says Tuka, my dear wife, what shall I do?
I don't know where to hide without paying my due.

(Tukaram: Dilip Chitre)

Advice to an Angry Wife: VII

I think about it and realize that
After all, this is His own kingdom.
Who would protect me from Him?
Where else can we go to escape Him?

The front yard is wide open and the backyard too.
In what stables or cowsheds can we hide?
His henchmen will chase us wherever we go.

I kick myself for becoming one of his share-croppers.
Now I can never get out of His clutches.

Says Tuka, it cannot be helped.
One has to remain here and live
On His terms – not our own.

(Tukaram: Dilip Chitre)

What profit will you get
out of hiding from me?
I'm right here, and I want you.

Those fantastic eyes – do you want to lock them in a bank?
You don't even raise your head to look at me.
Do you think you can invest that amazing smile at a good rate?
I can't get you to smile at me.

    What profit will you get?

Those towering breasts – are you going to put them in a vault?
You're hiding them under your sari.
Are you planning to hoard underground
the full bloom of your youth?
You keep so still under your veil.

    What profit will you get?

You want to stash away words instead of spending them in
                                  love?
You don't even move your lips.
You belong to me now, and I –
I'm God.
At last we can do business.

    What profit will you get?

(Annamacharya: V. Narayana Rao and David Shulman)

Gopal has slipped in and stolen my heart, friend.
He stole through my eyes and invaded my breast
    simply by looking—who knows how he did it?—
Even though parents and husband and all
    crowded the courtyard and filled my world.
The door was protected by all that was proper;
    not a corner, nothing, was left without a guard.
Decency, prudence, respect for the family—
    these three were locks and I hid the keys.
The sturdiest doors were my eyelid gates—
    to enter through them was a passage impossible—
And secure in my heart, a mountainous treasure:
    insight, intelligence, fortitude, wit.
And then, says Sur, he'd stolen it—
    with a thought and a laugh and a look—
        and my body was scorched with remorse.

(Surdas: John Stratton Hawley and Mark Juergensmeyer)

I'll go
to Girdhar's home

my true love
his beauty
ensnared me

I'll go
at night
come back
at dawn

play with him
all day
entice him

wear
what he wants
eat
what he gives

our love
is ancient
I can't stay away

I'll sit
where he says
let him sell me
if he wants

he is my master
I'll let him do
anything

(Mirabai: Rahul Soni)

'KRISHNA SUFFERS IN YOUR DESERTION'

God as Devotee, Debtor, Patient

Eating God

Ever since your name has entered Hari's ear
It's been "Radha, oh Radha," an infinite mantra,
    a formula chanted to a secret string of beads.
Nightly he sits by the Jumna, in a grove
    far from his friends and his happiness and home.
    He yearns for you. He has turned into a yogi:
    constantly wakeful, whatever the hour.
Sometimes he spreads himself a bed of tender leaves;
    sometimes he recites your treasurehouse of fames;
Sometimes he pledges silence: he closes his eyes
    and meditates on every pleasure of your frame—
His eye the invocation, his heart the oblation,
    his mutterings the food to feed
    the priests who tend the fire.
So has Syam's whole body wasted away.
    Says Sur, let him see you. Fulfill his desire.

           (Surdas: John Stratton Hawley and Mark Juergensmeyer)

Transfixed on Beauty

Transfixed on beauty's gem-like face
Shyamalo gazed upon her face
eye-contact exiled *vireh*'s longings.
His embrace made her half his body;

still fixed on beauty's gem-like face.

Arms round his neck she lauds him;
You're my sanctuary, he declares,
my splendour, my heart's adornment!
Their ecstatic minds in concert sway,

transfixed on beauty's gem-like face.

Flesh and spirit, soul and wealth—
all yours, believe me doe-eyed one.
My mouth forgets to kiss, beloved,
my heart is not forgetful, Love—

transfixed on beauty's gem-like face.

Krishna sings your paeans, bless'd one.
On him Shiva meditates.
Narsi's Swami is ocean's roar
Your mutual praise the ocean sings

transfixed on beauty's gem-like face.

(Narsinh Mehta: Keki Daruwalla and Meena Desai)

Lotus-eyed Krishna Longing for Love

"I'll stay here, you go to Radha!
Appease her with my words and bring her to me!"
Commanded by Madhu's foe, her friend
Went to repeat his words to Radha.

The Tenth Song

Sandalwood mountain winds blow,
Spreading passion.
Flowers bloom in profusion,
Tearing deserted lovers' hearts.
    Wildflower-garlanded Krishna
    Suffers in your desertion, friend.

Cool moon rays scorch him,
Threatening death.
Love's arrow falls
And he laments his weakness.
    Wildflower-garlanded Krishna
    Suffers in your desertion, friend.

Bees swarm, buzzing sounds of love,
Making him cover his ears.
Your neglect affects his heart,
Inflicting pain night after night.
    Wildflower-garlanded Krishna
    Suffers in your desertion, friend.

He dwells in dense forest wilds,
Rejecting his luxurious house.
He tosses on his bed of earth,
Frantically calling your name.
    Wildflower-garlanded Krishna
    Suffers in your desertion, friend.

Poet Jayadeva sings
To describes Krishna's desolation.
When your heart feels his strong desire,
Hari will rise to favour you.
    Wildflower-garlanded Krishna
    Suffers in your desertion, friend.

(Jayadeva: Barbara Stoler Miller)

In devotees' hearts, I build my home
and guard it with divine conch and whirl-blade,
the talismans of their faith.

Like a calf hungry for its mother's milk
I follow my disciples for their love.

Strung to their devotion like flowers on a thread,
I exist only in the garlands of their love.

For my family and friends
my heart sheds blood.

I did not hesitate to defend my followers at Hastina,
nor did I balk at eating a meal from humble Vidura's plate.

The blisters of their weight feel like balm to my shoulders
and how I long for them to kick me in mock fury.[1]

Says Salabega, a devotee from Islam,
my Vrindavan pilgrimage awaits the sanction of my Lord
                                                    at Puri.

(Salabega: Prabhanjan Mishra)

---

[1] A folk legend claims Radha once kicked out Krishna from her bed
and her action is lauded as the highest expression of devotional love.

Jana sweeps with a broom
The Lord loads up the garbage

Carries it in a basket on His head
Throws it away in a distant dump

So much under the spell of bhakti is He
He now performs the lowliest of tasks

Says Jani to Vithoba
How shall I return Your favours?

(Janabai: Dilip Chitre)

Among basil plants growing wild
Jani loosens her hair:

The Lord with butter in the palm of His hand
Gently massages her head:

"My poor little Jani has no one but me!"
He thinks as he pours down water:

Jani tells all the folks
"My boyfriend gives me a shower."

(Janabai: Dilip Chitre)

He's worn out. Bring him to me.
I'm the specialist in that disease.

Too many eyes have pierced him.
I may have to use love-charms, extra-strength.
His muscles are sore from battling breasts.
I'll massage him with a warm embrace.

   I'm the specialist.

He must be exhausted from so much loving.
I'll touch him with the herb that revives.
His sensitive parts have melted down.
I'll bring them to life
with charms of shyness.

   I'm the specialist.

Those artless women – how exciting can they be?
I have the right drug.
He's the handsome god on the hill,
and I'm Alamelumanga.
He's with me now. I can cure him.

   I'm the specialist.

   (Annamacharya: V. Narayana Rao and David Shulman)

'IF YOU CAN FIGURE IT OUT'

Twilight Tongues

Brother, I've seen some
    Astonishing sights:
A lion keeping watch
    Over pasturing cows;
A mother delivered
    After her son was;
A guru prostrated
    Before his disciple;
Fish spawning
    On treetops;
A cat carrying away
    A dog;
A gunnysack
    Driving a bullock cart;
A buffalo going out to graze,
    Sitting on a horse;
A tree with its branches in the earth,
    Its roots in the sky;
A tree with flowering roots.

This verse, says Kabir,
    Is your key to the universe.
If you can figure it out.

                            (Kabir: A.K. Mehrotra)

What is this untellable tale about?
The ogress and the dog make bedroom eyes;
The big cat prowls the jungle;
In my family of five, all hell breaks loose.
Led by drum-beating rabbits, a herd
Of antelopes mounts an attack;
The hunter's around, though all he does is watch.
The sea's ablaze, the forest's turned to ash,
But the fish are out looking for game.
The true pundit will get the story, says Kabir.
He's my guru. He'll save himself and save me too.

(Kabir: A.K. Mehrotra)

An ant flew into the sky,
She swallowed the sun.
That wasn't the only wonder:
The barren gave birth to a son.

The scorpion burrows into the underworld
On the head of the liberated one,
A cobra sits unfurled.
Unto a fly, a hawk is born.

Muktabai watches
Muktabai laughs.

(Muktabai: Jerry Pinto and Neela Bhagwat)

Onion and garlic are one, I've learnt.
Fry some onion. It's hardly a gourmet dish.
Fried onion, I wouldn't touch a sliver of it.
But it gave me a taste for saying, 'I am He.'

(Lal Ded: Ranjit Hoskote)

The deer with the tiger's head
The tiger with the deer's head
The two—joined at the waist—
It is not the tiger, not the deer
But something else
Come to eat next. Look!
When the body without the head
Grazes—
Look, O Gogeshwara,
The leaf vanishes.

(Allama Prabhu: H.S. Shivaprakash)

I saw, O Friend
A monkey fondling an elephant
That had dropped dead.
I saw, O Friend
A harlot in a forest calling men
And pawning herself.
I saw, O Friend
Dogs quarrelling in a ravaged town.
What is this wonder, O Gogeshwara?

(Allama Prabhu: H.S. Shivaprakash)

Ah!
A tiger came
From a desolate land
To eat my young calf
The tiger couldn't return
To the desolate land
The tiger looked at the young calf
And turned into a mother.
What shall I say of this?
O Kudalsangamadeva, dear to Ganga!

(Gangambike: H.S. Shivaprakash)

'YOUR BREATH IN MY BODY'

Seeker as Sought

He laughs when you laugh, sneezes in your sleep,
yawns for you, coughs for you.
He bathes every day in the river of your thoughts.
He's naked, all year round, and walks where you walk.
Just go up and introduce yourself.

(Lal Ded: Ranjit Hoskote)

Like treasure hiding in the earth
Like taste hiding in the fruit
Like gold hiding in the stone
Like oil hiding in sesame
Like fire hiding in the tree
No one can see Channamallikarjuna—
The Brahman hiding in yearning.

(Akka Mahadevi: H.S. Shivaprakash)

I'm no worshipper;
I'm no giver;
I'm not even a beggar,

  O lord
  without your grace.

Do it all yourself, my lord of the meeting rivers,
as a mistress would
when the maids are sick.

(Basavanna: A.K. Ramanujan)

I'm the one who has the body,
you're the one who holds the breath.

You know the secret of my body,
I know the secret of your breath.

That's why your body
is in mine.

You know
and I know, Ramanatha,

the miracle

of your breath
in my body.

(Devara Dasimayya: A.K. Ramanujan)

The essence of beauty
Springs from the eternal play
Of man as Krishna
And woman as Radha.
Devoted lovers
In the act of loving,
Seek to reach
The goal.
Who is devoted
To whom and how
Is of no interest.
Dedicate your soul
To the service of loving.
Love was born
To Radha
As one by one,
Her eight friends helped.
If your senses
And the mind
Can grasp the essence,
Krishna is reached.

Says Chandidas:
Listen, O brother man,
Man is the greatest Truth
Of all,
Nothing beyond.

(Chandidas: Deben Bhattacharya)

This is the big fight, King Ram.
Let anyone settle it who can.
Is Brahma bigger or where he came from?
Is the Veda bigger or where it was born from?
Is the mind bigger or what it believes in?
Is Ram bigger or the knower of Ram?
Kabir turns round, it's hard to see –
Is the holy place bigger, or the devotee?

(Kabir: Linda Hess and Shukdev Singh)

Now I have understood well
That One must become like Him
Whom One seeks:

You are beyond desire, O Narayana!
And I am just like You.

It is like a thief
Against the Master Thief:
Who will rob whom?
We are testing our skills.

Says Tuka, I fight with myself:
I fear no loss of life.

(Tukaram: Dilip Chitre)

'THERE CAN BE NO METAPHOR'

Words

Looking for your light,
I went out:

    it was like the sudden dawn
    of a million million suns,

    a ganglion of lightnings
    for my wonder.

    O Lord of Caves,
    if you are light,
    there can be no metaphor.

                    (Allama Prabhu: A.K. Ramanujan)

To arrange words
In some order
Is not the same thing
As the inner poise
That's poetry.

The truth of poetry
Is the truth
Of being.
It's an experience
Of truth.

No ornaments
Survive.
A crucible.
Fire reveals
Only molten
Gold.

Says Tuka
We are here
To reveal.
We do not waste
Words.

(Tukaram: Dilip Chitre)

Where does one begin with you?
O Lord, you have no opening line.
It's so hard to get you started.

Everything I tried went wrong.
You've used up all my faculties.

What I just said vanished in the sky
And I've fallen to the ground again.

Says Tuka, my mind is stunned:
I can't find a word to say.

(Tukaram: Dilip Chitre)

She Said:
The texts of philosophy may speak
of his colour, his ornaments, his beauty,
his names, his forms . . .
although they hold aloft
the bright light of lofty knowledge everywhere
they still cannot see
the greatness of my lord.

(Nammalvar: Archana Venkatesan)

A thousand times at least I asked my Guru
to give Nothingness a name.
Then I gave up. What name can you give
to the source from which all names have sprung?

(Lal Ded: Ranjit Hoskote)

Isn't it funny
That though she's Mother of the Universe,

we warble
about her lotus-bud breasts
and her eyes more limpid than a doe's?

And though she has no beginning or end
we hail her as the little girl born
to the Monarch of the Great Mountain?

Hilarious really
all the hyperbole

when she's beyond it all –
description, explanation,

perception.

(Abhirami Bhattar: Arundhathi Subramaniam)

'THE LORD IS AS IF HE WERE NOT'

Breakthrough, Endgame

The wind sleeps
to lullabies of sky.

Space drowses,
infinity gives it suck
from her breast.

The sky is silent.
The lullaby is over.

The Lord is
as if He were not.

(Allama Prabhu: A.K. Ramanujan)

The Lord has entered my being.
I make pilgrimage within myself and am purified.
I met Him.
He found me good
And let me lose myself in Him.
'Beloved! If you find me fair
My pilgrimage is made,
I am cleansed.
More than the sacred waters of Ganga, Yamuna
    and Tribeni mingled at the Sangam;
More than the seven seas,
More than charity, almsgiving and prayer
Is the knowledge of Eternity that is the Lord.'

Nanak says: he who has worshipped the Great Giver of life
        Has earned more merit than those who
        bathe at the sixty and eight places of pilgrimage.

(Guru Nanak: Khushwant Singh)

209

That actor Nagar[1] has come in disguise
Opened a shop filled with impish tricks
Saints have unmasked him
Have hurled his weighing scale and measures
     Into the flowing river.

         (Sami: Mohan Gehani and Menka Shivdasani)

He is a true trader who has brought riches home,
Who, in trust, has exchanged his heart with the Beloved,
Who dishonours none
Who believes this world to be transient,

     Like a dream.

         (Sami: Mohan Gehani and Menka Shivdasani)

---

[1] *Nagar*: another name of Krishna

Fire, fire! The town in flames!
    But it's no bane
    to denizens of the air
    freely flying.

It's the rats
    that scurry and shriek!
    All those too weak
    to take to the air.

Akha says,
    the seer is not shaken
    by phenomena.
    He navigates the sky
    on practiced wings.

(Akho: Gieve Patel)

Wrapped up in Yourself, You hid from me.
All day I looked for You
And when I found You hiding inside me,
I ran wild, playing now me, now You.

(Lal Ded: Ranjit Hoskote)

In the infinite dark,
Who placed the inordinate light,
Its opposite?
Darkness is
Light
Is
Itself—
The same!
There!
What kind of marvel is this?
One is not afraid of the other.

Seeing
The elephant and the lion
Together
Feeding
I was amazed,
O Gogeshwara.

(Allama Prabhu: H.S. Shivaprakash)

If they see
breasts and long hair coming
they call it woman,

if beard and whiskers
they call it man:

but, look, the self that hovers
in between
is neither man
nor woman

O Ramanatha

(Devara Dasimayya: A.K. Ramanujan)

Horizontal He is:
He is vertical.
Down and across
One intense light.

God is not uniform:
What makes Him
Homogeneous
Is purity of the heart.

Arguments about
His unity or duality
Are condemned
To continue.

Says Tuka,
You must come
Out of your involvements
And vested interests
To grasp Him
Whole.

(Tukaram: Dilip Chitre)

I sense him here. My God. From the temple. Here.
In my home. The roof has flown off.
I am open to the sky.

Until this happens to you, you're condemned
To play out those old roles of the ego.
You're going to live in those old illusions
And wonder why nothing works as it should.

Welcome to maya.

Muktai offers this milk of instruction:
One God: every possible emotional state.

(Muktabai: Jerry Pinto and Neela Bhagwat)

If I say one, it isn't so.
If I say two, it's slander.
Kabir has thought about it.
As it is,
so it is.

(Kabir: Linda Hess and Shukdev Singh)

'SUNRISE IS SUNSET'

Ecstasy

I wore myself out, looking for myself.
No one could have worked harder to break the code.
I lost myself in myself and found a wine cellar. Nectar,
                                        I tell you.
There were jars and jars of the good stuff, and no one to
                                        drink it.

(Lal Ded: Ranjit Hoskote)

I, Lalla, came through the gate of my soul's jasmine garden
and found Shiva and Shakti there, locked in love!
Drunk with joy, I threw myself into the lake of nectar.
Who cares if I'm a dead woman walking!

(Lal Ded: Ranjit Hoskote)

Such happiness then, such happiness.
I could have sat there even to the end.
I bathed in the Indrayani and joy-soaked
I went to the temple. I looked upon
Panduranga. I felt his gaze on me.

The words began to flow.

I bowed to Tukoba and went home.

Bahini says: the ocean is within me,
In the sky of my heart, God spoke in thunder.

(Bahinabai: Jerry Pinto and Neela Bhagwat)

Blue is this sky blue is this space filled with love
Blue is this entire symmetry
Blue is Being-in-Itself blue is the colour of karma
Blue is one's Guru and one's Guru's resort
I behave blue I feed on blue
I become blue I envision blue
Jnanadeva has come into the school of blue
In the loving and sensuous embrace of blue

(Jnaneshwar: Dilip Chitre)

When
like a hailstone crystal
like a waxwork image
the flesh melts in pleasure
    how can I tell you?

The waters of joy
broke the banks
and ran out of my eyes.

I touched and joined
my lord of the meeting rivers.
How can I talk to anyone
of that?

(Basavanna: A.K. Ramanujan)

God of my clan,
I'll not place my feet
But where your feet
Have stood before:
I've no feet
of my own.

How can the immoralists
of this world know
the miracle, that oneness
of your feet
and mine,

Ramanatha?

(Devara Dasimayya: A.K. Ramanujan)

Bliss soured to become the cream of bliss.
Blessed, I've begun to churn the cream.

My body rocks and sways in bliss.
My arms are lost, my eyes are lost.

Look! How Narayana gathers up Himself!
Look! How He transforms His properties!

Says Tuka, He is reaching the brim now!
In an instant, He is going to overflow!

(Tukaram: Dilip Chitre)

In a torrent of love, reason drowned.
Sami would not live without seeing Him.
What the sages spoke of,
I saw in an instant!

(Sami: Mohan Gehani and Menka Shivdasani)

The word 'love' taught me by my Sadguru
Has cleansed my heart.
Sami says, in a moment He set on fire all doubts,
Hoisted me aloft and I could see

Everything!

(Sami: Mohan Gehani and Menka Shivdasani)

Water has turned
Into the sky.
One has lapsed
Into all.

How to contain it now?
It ripples in itself.

What can spill out of it?
It has closed up itself.

Says Tuka,
This is
The end of the world
Sunrise is sunset.

(Tukaram: Dilip Chitre)

He grabbed me
    lest I go astray.

Wax before an unspent fire
    mind melted,
      body trembled.

I bowed, I wept,
    danced, and cried aloud,
      I sang, and I praised him.

Unyielding, as they say,
  as an elephant's jaw
  or a woman's grasp
  was love's unrelenting
  seizure.

Love pierced me
  like a nail
      driven into a green tree.

Overflowing, I tossed
  like a sea,

heart growing tender,
body shivering,

while the world called me Demon!
and laughed at me,

I left shame behind,

took as an ornament
    the mockery of local folk.
Unswerving, I lost my cleverness
    In the bewilderment of ecstasy.

(Manikkavacakar: A.K. Ramanujan)

'WE HAVE SLAIN EACH OTHER'

Liberation

I won't come
I won't go
I won't live
I won't die

I'll keep uttering
The name
And lose myself
In it

I'm bowl
And I'm platter
I'm man
And I'm woman

I'm grapefruit
And I'm sweet lime
I'm Hindu
And I'm Muslim

I'm fish
And I'm net
I'm fisherman
And I'm time

I'm nothing
Says Kabir
I'm not among the living
Or the dead

(Kabir: A.K. Mehrotra)

I'm nothing
A nobody
Native
Of nowhere
I am alone
In my own place

I do not visit
Any place
I neither come
Nor go
I talk
To emptiness

Nobody
Belongs to me
I belong
To nobody
None of this
Is true

I do not
Have to live
I do not
Have to die
I am
Undivided

Says Tuka
I have no name
Or form
I am neither active
Nor passive

(Tukaram: Dilip Chitre)

He knows the crown is the temple of Self.
His breath is deepened by the Unstruck Sound.
He has freed himself from the prison of delusion.
He knows he is God, who shall he worship?

(Lal Ded: Ranjit Hoskote)

When the camphor hill catches fire
Does the charcoal remain?
Does the snow-built Shiva temple
Have a sunlight cupola?
When a hill of cinders is shot
With a wax arrow
Why look for the arrow again?
After seeing Gogeshwara
Why remember him again?

(Allama Prabhu: H.S. Shivaprakash)

One colour now, one colour, you and me.
I look at you, Panduranga, one look, no you, no me.

Those passions quieten.

The body is.

The body withers.

One now, no me, no you.

Soyara says: Who's being seen?
    Who's doing the seeing?

(Soyarabai: Jerry Pinto and Neela Bhagwat)

Everybody understands
    the single drop merging into the ocean.

One in a million comprehends
    the ocean merging in a single drop.

(Kabir: Vinay Dharwadker)

He: neither line nor form,
    Body: absent. Ground: groundless.

Behold the bodiless man, standing in the middle of
    the circle of the sky.

                      (Kabir: Vinay Dharwadker)

For me God is dead.
Let him be for those who need him.

I shall speak of him no more.
I shall not name him again.

We have slain each other.

In his praise, I cursed him.
Lord, what an endless affair!

Says Tuka, I have squandered my whole life after him.
Now I would like to sit still.

                    (Tukaram: Dilip Chitre)

Acknowledgements

I am grateful for a Homi Bhabha Fellowship that gave me what poet-anthologists yearn for, most of all: licence to read.

My sincerest thanks to the following:

To theatre stalwart and friend, the late Satyadev Dubey, who orchestrated the Fellowship application process from his hospital bed with a maestro's panache.

To Prof. S.M. Chitre and H.D. Pajnigar of the Homi Bhabha Fellowships Council for their support.

To Kamini Mahadevan, my editor at Penguin, for mooting the idea, and for being a perceptive and gentle fellow-traveller.

To Adil Jussawalla and Gieve Patel for believing in the project, for affirmation and encouragement.

To Ranjit Hoskote for believing in it too, for solidarity, for dialogue.

To Jerry Pinto for intuition, laughter, bibliophilia.

Acknowledgements

To Rudi Heredia and Priya D'Souza for faith and friendship.

To P.R. Umamaheshwaran for his patient and skilful textual unravelling, and 'Marabin Maindan' Muthiah for opening up the world of *Abhirami Antadi* for me in its many textures, for his contagious passion for the work.

To the many poets and translators who are in this book. To many who are not. And to the many people who played significant roles behind the scenes, sometimes without knowing it: Viju Chitre, Dhruba Hazarika, Naushil Mehta, Hemant Divate, K. Satchidanandan, Arvind Krishna Mehrotra, Udayan Vajpeyi, Satyasheel Deshpande, Shoba Ghosh, David Shulman, Lata Mani, Maa Karpoori.

To Sadhguru, for opening my eyes to the fact that I am, however flawed, a bhakta, above all else.

Notes on Poets

Abhirami Bhattar was a priest of the Thirukadaiyur temple, on the east coast of Tamil Nadu, and preeminent Tamil poet of the goddess Abhirami. He lived during the eighteenth and early nineteenth centuries, and his ferocious bhakti led many to consider him mad. The story goes that he irked the King Serfoji with his goddess-intoxicated proclamation that it was a full moon day (when it was actually a new moon). The king ordered that he be beheaded if the moon did not rise that night. Abhirami Bhattar lit a large fire and erected a platform over it, tied with ropes. He sat on the platform, spontaneously singing verses in praise of Goddess Abhirami. With each verse, he cut off one rope. On completing the seventy-ninth hymn, Abhirami appeared and threw her diamond earring skywards so that it shone like the full moon. This was the legendary genesis of the *Abhirami Antadi*, an inspired collection of a hundred hymns.

Akho (1591–1656) was a medieval Gujarati Bhakti poet and a goldsmith by profession. He is known for his pungent satirical poetry written in a verse pattern he introduced called the *chhappa*. He migrated from Jetalpur to Ahmedabad, where he lived much of his life. It is held that he accepted Gokulnath, grandson of Vallabhacharya, as his master, but his verse reveals a strong philosophically non-dualist impulse. Although he never renounced the path of bhakti, there is a deep impatience with hypocrisy, ritual and sentiment, and a predisposition towards the path of knowledge and renunciation that asserts itself time and again in his verse.

Akka Mahadevi was a twelfth-century mystic poet and wandering ascetic associated with the Sharana movement of Karnataka. A younger contemporary of Basavanna and Allama Prabhu, she betrothed herself to Lord Shiva as Chennamallikarjuna at an early age, and is said to have renounced family life and worldly attachment, shedding even her clothes in the process. Her 400-odd vachana poems are considered a significant contribution to Kannada Bhakti literature. She found acceptance and refuge in Kalyana at the community founded by Basavanna, but after a time resumed the life of a wandering ascetic. She is believed to have died young, leaving behind a legacy of poetry that speaks lyrically of various psychological and existential states—illicit love, love in union and love in separation—often in the course of a single poem.

Allama Prabhu was a mystic saint and poet of twelfth-century Karnataka, whose suffix Prabhu, Master, suggests the high esteem in which he was held as spiritual preceptor. Dismissive of all form of external ritual and worship, he was the presiding spiritual authority of the Anubhava Mantapa (Mansion of Experience) established by Basavanna for fellow Sharanas. Several of the 1300-odd vachanas attributed to him are characterized by their cryptic, riddle-like language, largely evocative of mystical realization rather than spiritual longing. A vivid legend tells of his encounter with a Siddha or adept who challenged him to sever his body in two. When Allama swung his sword, it encountered a yogically invulnerable body, and not a hair on the adept's body was touched. But when the Siddha did the same, the sword simply passed through Allama's form as if it were thin air. The distinction between occult virtuosity and true enlightenment was established.

Annamacharya or Annamayya was a saint-poet of the fifteenth century whose devotional poetry is regarded as one of the finest achievements of classical Telugu literature. He lived at the hilltop shrine of Tirupati in Andhra Pradesh, and is said to have composed a song a day for the god of the temple. He spearheaded a new genre of love poetry, the short *padam*, which left its indelible mark on the Carnatic music tradition. His poems addressed to Lord Venkatesha were inscribed on copper plates and stored in the Tirupati temple vault. They reveal two dominant modes of bhakti: *adhyatma* and *shringara*, or the metaphysical/ introspective and the erotic.

Andal ('the one who rules') was a ninth-century woman mystic, famous for the fierce bridal mysticism of her verse. The only woman among the twelve Alvar or Vaishnava saint-poets, her *Tiruppavai* and *Nachiyar Tirumozhi* are considered masterpieces of Tamil literature. According to legend, the young Andal was convinced she was betrothed to Lord Krishna, and adorned herself daily with a garland meant for the temple deity. Her father discovered a strand of her hair in the garland, and was horrified at this act of desecration. That night, the Lord appeared to him in a dream, insisting that the only garland that appealed to him was one made fragrant by Andal's hair. Eventually, a jubilant procession carried the fifteen-year-old Andal, dressed in bridal finery, to the Srirangam temple where she dissolved into her beloved Lord Ranganatha, attaining immortality as one of the greatest women mystics in history.

Appar (literally 'father') or Tirunavukkarasar was one of the most prominent of the sixty-three Nayanmar or Tamil Shaiva poet-saints. He lived in the seventh century and was an elder contemporary of the other great Shaiva devotee, Sambandar, who conferred upon him the epithet 'father'. Born in Tiruvamur in Tamil Nadu, Appar was drawn to Jainism early in life and joined a Jain monastery. However, when he fell seriously ill, he returned home, at his sister's behest, and prayed at a local Shiva temple, after which he was miraculously cured. This marked his conversion, and he spent the rest of his life travelling to various southern temples and singing songs of praise. He composed thousands of hymns called the *Tevaram*, in which he sang of his conversion to a religion of love, and the joy and surprise of being ambushed by Shiva.

Bahinabai (1628–1700) was a poet and devout Vithoba follower. Her autobiographical work, *Atmanivedana*, discloses an account of her early marriage, her troubled marital life as well as her deepening devotion to Lord Vithoba of Pandharpur. The poet Tukaram apparently appeared to her in visions, and initiated her into a form of mantra worship; thereafter, she considered him her guru. Although her husband never understood her spiritual aspirations, she remained committed to her relationship until the end of her life. Many of her poems or abhangas dwell on the conflict between the demands of her familial life and her love of Vithoba, as well as the challenges of being born a woman in an inegalitarian society.

Basavanna or Basaveshwara was a mystic, teacher, poet, social reformer and statesman of the twelfth century. He was a proponent of equality across the barriers of gender, caste, class and religion, and a leading figure of the Virashaiva Sharana movement. Born into a Brahmin family in Bagewadi, he grew disenchanted with the rigidity of his socio-religious environment early in life. He found a spiritual guide in Kudalasangama, and forged a deep connect with the deity of Shiva at the local temple. Later, he entered public life, becoming Finance Minister to the Chalukyan king at Kalyana. A charismatic spiritual leader, Basavanna founded a community for fellow-Sharanas, based on egalitarian ideals, which became the nucleus of a remarkable galaxy of saints and mendicant devotees. He left behind a great legacy of vachana poetry, celebrated for its insight and virtuoso command of metaphor and rhythm.

Chandidas was a fifteenth-century poet and mystic considered, in the words of his translator Deben Bhattacharya, to be 'the father of Bengali poetry'. His *Srikrishnakirtan*, a body of 1250 poems in praise of the amorous exploits of Radha and Krishna, is considered to be a masterpiece of medieval Bengali literature. The legend of Chandidas—a Brahmin priest who fell in love with a low-caste washerwoman, Rami, and became the scandal of the village—is a well-known one. The forbidden passion and volatile emotional relationship between Radha and Krishna in Chandidas's poems, as well as his defiant rejection of 'all laws/ made by man or god' on the path of love, is in the mode of Sahaja Bhakti—an affirmation of the role of the body and the five senses on the spiritual journey.

Chokhamela was a Maharashtrian Varkari saint-poet who lived during the late thirteenth and early fourteenth century. He belonged to the Mahar caste, which was considered untouchable at the time. He lived with his wife, Soyarabai, and his son, Karmamela, in Mangalvedha. His devotion to Lord Vithoba was further fueled by the kirtan and teaching of his contemporary, Namdev. There are legendary tales of Lord Vithoba intervening to help his devotee in his hereditary task of carrying animal carcasses from people's homes and disposing of them outside town limits. It is said that when Chokhamela died in a construction accident, Namdev rushed to his village and identified his friend's body because even his bones murmured the name of Vitthal. These were buried near the steps of the Pandharpur temple. Chokhamela is believed to have left behind a legacy of over 200 poems or abhangas.

Chowdaiah, the ferryman, was a Kannada vachana poet of the artisan class. Among these compelling voices from the excluded sections of the caste hierarchy (as scholar H.S. Shivaprakash tells us) were those of woodcutters, washermen, toddy-tappers, cowherds, rice-gatherers, town-criers, and even burglars! The poetry of Ambigara Chowdaiah is infused by the rage and rebellion of one who has a deep first-hand experience of caste humiliation. These voices from areas of traditional caste relegation brought a new variety of form and vitality of tone to the realm of Kannada Bhakti poetry.

Devara Dasimayya was a tenth-century mystic and among the earliest of the vachana poets of the Sharana movement in Karnataka. Born in Mudanaru, he is supposed to have performed austere penance in a dense forest until his beloved god, Shiva, appeared before him and advised him to give up a life of self-flagellation and worship him through a life of engagement with the world. This marked a turning point, and Dasimayya became a weaver, although his devotion did not abate. There are several legends of him initiating diverse groups to the path of Virashaivism, from local tribals and orthodox Vaishnava Brahmins to the queen of the Chalukya kingdom, and eventually the king and his subjects as well. His vachana poems (approximately 150 in number, addressed to Lord Ramanatha or Shiva as the Lord of Rama) are characterized by their homespun metaphors, brevity and aphoristic precision.

Dhoolaiah, the cobbler, was a vachana poet of the Virashaiva tradition and belonged, like many of his poet compatriots, to the artisan class. As a cobbler, he belonged to the lowest echelons of the caste hierarchy. Significantly, however, as his translator H.S. Shivaprakash points out, the medieval Sharana movement emerged from the grassroots, and had its firm basis in the rejection of a caste-based inequality. In one of his poems, the cobbler even dismisses Lord Shiva when he chooses to visit at an inopportune moment, distracting Dhoolaiah from his immersion in sandal-making. 'Go, go away,' the cobbler declares dismissively in a poem that becomes an assertion of the dignity of his profession, and an affirmation of the meditative absorption that it offered.

Gangambike was a significant woman poet of the Kannada vachana tradition. She also happened to be one of the wives of Basavanna, the legendary mystic reformer of the twelfth century. Along with his other wife, Nilambike, and his elder sister, Nagalambike, she played an active role in furthering the cause of the Virashaiva Sharana movement that he spearheaded. Translator H.S. Shivaprakash points out that the spotlight on the work of Akka Mahadevi, the most celebrated woman mystic of the tradition, often sidelines the work of other important women poets of the time.

Guru Nanak (1469–1539) was the founder of the Sikh faith, the first of the ten Sikh gurus, and one of the major devotional poets of northern India whose sacred revelatory compositions in praise of the formless Absolute is contained in the *Adi Granth*, the holy text of the Sikhs. Drawing on the mystical legacies of Hinduism and Islam, Guru Nanak elevated reality (*sat*) to the position of the One Supreme God, and emphasized the importance of bhakti through the worship of the name of God (*Nama Marga*). After a mystical experience at the age of thirty, he spent the rest of his years travelling widely, singing and composing hymns and preaching the oneness of the divine across dogmatic boundaries of creed.

Janabai was a Marathi bhakti poet of the thirteenth century, who is believed to have composed over three hundred poems in praise of Vithoba. Born into a Shudra family, she lost her mother early, after which her father took her to Pandharpur where she worked as a maidservant in the house of Damsheti and Gonai, the parents of the saint-poet, Namdev. Janabai attended to Namdev for many years, and regarded him not merely as an employer but as a guru. Despite being unlettered, she composed verse of a high calibre, many of her abhangas visualizing Vithoba not just as mother, but as maidservant (affectionately termed Vitthalabai). In her verse, Vitthala often favours his ardent devotee by performing her household chores.

Jayadeva was the twelfth-century author of the *Gita Govinda*, a celebrated dramatic-lyrical poem in Sanskrit, and a highly influential work in Vaishnava mystical literature, inspiring Bhakti poets for centuries thereafter. Focusing on Krishna's love of Radha in a series of twelve cantos, these erotic-spiritual songs constitute an important part of the devotional literature of Orissa, Bengal and South India. While there are varied versions of his biography, most sources agree that Jayadeva was born in eastern India in a Brahmin family; he was a poet and a brilliant student of Sanskrit, but soon turned to the life of a wandering mendicant. Legend has it that his relationship with the temple dancer Padmavati, who shared his devotion towards Lord Jagannatha of Puri, was one of the inspirations for the *Gita Govinda*.

Jnaneshwar was a thirteenth-century poet, mystic, yogi of the Nath tradition, and founder of the Varkari movement. His major literary works, *Bhavarth Deepika* or *Jnaneshwari* (a commentary on the *Bhagavad Gita* composed in the ovimetre) and *Amrutanubhav*, are considered landmarks of Marathi literature. He also composed several abhangas in praise of Krishna. He and his siblings were orphaned early when their ostracized parents committed suicide. According to a wonderful legend, he stunned an orthodox Brahmin community by miraculously getting a buffalo to recite the Vedas! That incident, which effortlessly established his point that god existed in the seemingly lowliest creature, marked the end of the family's ostracism. He is said to have shed his body, taking *sanjeevan samadhi*, at the age of twenty-one. His shrine in the town of Alandi draws thousands of pilgrims to this day.

Kabir (a weaver by profession) was a North Indian mystic poet of the fifteenth century whose poems—with their emphasis on a direct relationship with the divine and impatience with orthodoxy—have been sung and recited by millions down the centuries. Born in Varanasi to a weaver class recently converted to Islam, he seems to have had a Hindu guru, and is celebrated for his abrasive social comment and stout opposition to dogmatic strains in both Hinduism and Islam. Popular legend has it that both Hindu and Muslim followers quarrelled over who should take charge of his body after his death, but their combat was interrupted by the discovery that the shroud contained not a body, but a heap of flowers. The fragrance lives on.

Kanhopatra was a fifteenth-century Marathi mystic poet in the Varkari movement or Vitthal tradition of Pandharpur. She is believed to have been a courtesan or dancer of considerable beauty who chose eventually to surrender her life at the feet of her beloved Lord Vithoba, the deity of Pandharpur, rather than become a concubine of the king of Bidar. Around thirty of her abhangas have survived. She is believed to be the only female Varkari saint without a guru; her strength of devotion alone is believed to have granted her mukti or liberation. She is also the only saint whose samadhi shrine lies within the precincts of the temple of Pandharpur.

Karaikal Ammaiyar was one of the three women mystics among the sixty-three Nayanmar or Tamil Shaiva saints and a significant figure in Tamil literature. Born in Karaikal in Tamil Nadu, she evinced a passionate devotion towards Shiva at an early age, which later deepened, turning apparently even her husband into her devotee. Legend has it that she made a pilgrimage to Mount Kailash (and later to Thiruvalangadu) in response to summons from her beloved Lord. But unwilling to taint the holy terrain with her feet, she preferred to walk on her hands rather than her feet—an image treasured by bhaktas down the ages as proof of a fierce and fiery devotion.

Kshetrajna or Kshetrayya was a prolific Telugu poet and composer of the seventeenth century. His erotic love poetry, in the padam tradition, expresses his devotion to Lord Krishna as Muvva Gopala (Muvva was the name of his native village). Unlike the padams of Annamacharya which were addressed to Lord Venkatesha of Tirupati, Kshetrayya's songs were probably invocations to god as well as to the royal patrons of his time, marking an important transitional moment in Telugu literary culture, where the king was identified with the deity (as A.K. Ramanujan, V. Narayana Rao and David Shulman explain). His padams constitute an integral part of the classical dance and music of South India to this very day.

Lal Ded is the best-known spiritual and literary figure of Kashmir, venerated for over seven centuries, as Lallesvari or Lalla Yogini by Hindus and Lal-'arifa by Muslims. Her 258 poems or *vakhs* mark the beginnings of modern Kashmiri literature. She lived in the fourteenth century, and is believed to have died in 1373. Born into a Brahmin family, she married at the age of twelve and led a difficult domestic life, facing incomprehension for her spiritual inclinations, and abused by her husband and mother-in-law. At the age of twenty-six, she renounced her home, became the disciple of a Shaiva guru, before taking to the life of a wandering mendicant—'not an easy choice for a Brahmin woman in fourteenth-century Kashmir', as her translator Ranjit Hoskote writes. Her vakhs remain her living legacy, still loved by Kashmiris across affiliations of faith and creed.

Lalon Fakir (1774–1890) was a mystic poet and the most celebrated figure in the Bengali Baul tradition of sacred troubadours or 'god's vagabonds'. A combination of Tantra, Sufism, yoga and Vaishnava devotion seems to have fuelled the mysticism of these self-professed 'madmen' who sing so hauntingly of the 'moner manush', the man of the heart. Little is known of Lalon Fakir's life other than the fact that he lived in Cheouria village in the Kushtia district of modern-day Bangladesh where he founded his group of like-minded minstrels. The scornful repudiation of narrow creedal affiliation, religious and communal intolerance, caste and class inequity, evinced in his poems, have made him a counter-cultural icon, whose influence can be seen in modern writers ranging from Tagore to Kazi Nazrul Islam and Allen Ginsberg.

Manikkavacakar was a ninth-century Tamil poet, considered one of the most significant Shiva saints, although he is not included among the sixty-three Nayanmars. Born to Brahmin parents, he travelled from one southern temple to another, and eventually settled in Chidambaram. Legend has it that when he was minister to the Pandya king, he was given money to purchase horses for the king's cavalry, but the god-crazed devotee built a temple in Tirupperunturai instead! Thankfully, Shiva intervened, and the king had a timely change of heart. Manikkavacakar's still-popular devotional poems are collected in the *Tiruvacakam*. A traditional proverb proclaims: 'He whose heart is not melted by the *Tiruvacakam* must have a stone for a heart.'

Mirabai (1498–1547) is one of the most significant figures of the Vaishnava Bhakti movement. Born into a Rajput family in Merta, Rajasthan, her passionate love for her Lord started early. Legends of her fraught familial life after her marriage are legion; it is believed that her beloved 'Dark One' stepped in miraculously to foil more than one attempt by her in-laws to murder her. She eventually abandoned her life of privilege, defied a conservative establishment and took to the streets, joining her true community of fellow bhaktas. Her bhajans of despair and ecstatic union with Giridhara Gopala (Krishna) have been translated worldwide and continue to be among the most popular bhajans sung in India.

Muktabai was a revered mystic and adept. Born in Maharashtra into a clan of spiritual luminaries, she was the youngest sibling of Nivrutti, Jnaneshwar and Sopan, a family responsible for establishing the Varkari tradition. A highly intelligent and accomplished yogini, she composed deeply philosophical, dense, esoteric verse, remarkably devoid of allusion to her personal life. She was revered in her time, becoming the spiritual guide of the Tantric yogi, Changdev, who was clearly much older than she was. She was also supposedly responsible for instructing the potter Gora Kumbhar to 'test' Namdev for his spiritual maturity; when he was proved 'half-baked', he sought refuge in Lord Vithoba who directed him to a guru under whom he became fully enlightened. She attained *mahasamadhi* at the incredibly young age of eighteen.

Namdev was one of the foremost poets of the Varkari tradition, and a contemporary of the saint Jnaneshwar. Born to a low-caste family in the thirteenth century, he was the son of Damsheti, a tailor, and Gonai. His fervent devotion to Vithoba started early, and his unworldly bent of mind made him the despair of his parents, wife and relatives. His Marathi *sankirtanas*, many of which asserted the irrelevance of caste on the spiritual path, won him a wide following among women, 'low' castes, and all those traditionally excluded from the religious life. He is considered a bhagat or holy man in the Sikh tradition as well. According to legend, he took a vow that he would compose a billion poems for Lord Vitthal—an impossible task that made him appear in the poet Tukaram's dream three centuries later and instruct him to complete the unfinished project!

Nammalvar (literally 'our own alvar') was regarded as the greatest of the twelve alvar or Tamil poets in the Vaishnava tradition, and his images are to be found in many South Indian temples. Born into a peasant caste, he lived between the ninth and tenth centuries, and composed four major literary works, of which the 1102 verses of the *Tiruvaymoli* are considered the most important. According to legend, he was mute from the time of his birth, and burst into speech when he encountered a poet and scholar from North India, Maturakavi (who followed a light in the southern sky until he reached Kurukur where Nammalvar lived). A.K. Ramanujan describes his poems as 'philosophic and poetic, direct in feeling yet intricate in design'—important in laying the foundations of later Vaishnava poetry.

Narsinh Mehta was a fifteenth-century Vaishnava poet-saint, considered to be the Adi Kavi or first poet of Gujarati literature. Born to a Nagar Brahmin family, Narsinh Mehta grew up in straitened circumstances. According to legend, an insult directed at him by his cousin's wife drove him to a nearby forest where he fasted and meditated for seven days. Lord Shiva appeared before him, and at the poet's request, took him to Vrindavan where he witnessed the grandeur of the raas leela of Krishna and the gopis. He spent the rest of his life singing Lord Krishna's praises, and left behind a legacy of kirtans that are sung even today. His early works are primarily richly erotic poems about Radha and Krishna, while his later literature turned more metaphysical.

Nivruttinath was a thirteenth-century saint-poet in the Varkari tradition. He was the eldest sibling in a spiritually exceptional family that comprised Jnaneshwar, Sopan and Muktabai—all acknowledged as celebrated mystics in their own right. Initiated into the Nath tradition, he was a guru to his siblings, and was responsible for instructing his younger brother, Jnaneshwar, to translate the Bhagavad Gita from Sanskrit into Marathi; the result was the *Jnaneshwari*, one of the greatest sacred works in Marathi literature. Nivruttinath voluntarily shed his body, attaining *mahasamadhi* in the holy town of Tryambakeshwar.

Puntanam Namboodiri (1547–1640) was a devotee of the Lord of Guruvayur and the author of a much-loved Malayalam work, *Jnanappana* (Song of Wisdom), sung by millions in Kerala even today. He lived in the area around Malappuram Kerala. Legend has it that he invited everyone in the village to a ritual to celebrate the birth of his son, but lost his infant on that very day. Heartbroken, he turned to Lord Guruvayurappan for consolation; the result was a moving collection of verses that became the *Jnanappana*. He was a contemporary of the other great devotee and author of the *Narayaneeyam*, Melpathur Narayana Bhattatiri. But it is said that Lord Guruvayurappan preferred Puntanam's simple, heartfelt verse to the former's scholarly Sanskrit and actually made his opinion known from the sanctum, asserting that bhakti was dearer to him than *vibhakti*!

Rahim (1556–1626) or Abdul Rahim Khan-e-Khana was a poet and one of the nine gems or luminaries in the court of Emperor Akbar. His name derives from the village of Khankhana, located in the Nawanshah district of Punjab. Although a Muslim by birth, he was a devotee of Lord Krishna—testimony to the tremendous spirit of cultural integration of the times—and is well known for his superbly crafted couplets dedicated to him. Well-versed in Sanskrit, he is famed for his couplets and books on astrology; he also translated the *Baburnama* into Persian.

Rajai was a woman poet in the Varkari tradition of Maharashtra who lived during the thirteenth and fourteenth centuries. She was the wife of Namdev, the major mystic poet, and several of her abhangas (as also those of his mother, Gonai) reveal her frustration at living with an unworldly householder. Born into the Shudra caste, she and Namdev had four sons, Nara, Vitha, Gonda and Mahada and a daughter, Limbai. The tradition abounds with stories of Lord Vithoba intervening to save her family from penury at crucial moments in her life.

Ramprasad Sen was a Shakta poet, saint and Tantric adept of eighteenth-century Bengal whose widely translated poems to goddess Kali, known as *Ramprasadi*, continue to be sung in Bengal. Born in the village of Halisar, he revealed an early poetic and spiritual inclination, and his discipleship under a Tantric yogi intensified his bhakti, producing a compositional form that integrated the Bengali folk style with classical melody and devotional kirtan. Many of these poems are in the mode of 'nindastuti'—an intimate praise poem or prayer through complaint and criticism, truculence and tantrum. An account of him scribbling love poems to Kali in the account books during his stint as a clerk with a Calcutta merchant offers an evocative image of his devotion. He eventually submerged himself in the river near Halisar on Kali Puja and became one with his beloved goddess.

Ravidas was a North Indian mystic, a contemporary of Kabir, who lived on the outskirts of Varanasi in the fifteenth century. Born into the chamar caste of tanners and leather workers, his songs defiantly proclaim his low caste and assert that spiritual progress alone confers true status. The idealized city of

'Begumpura'—a land without sorrow—is invoked in his work as one free of caste prejudice and impoverishment. The oral tradition records his meetings with fellow saints: Kabir, Mirabai, Nanak, Gorakhnath and Ramanand. His poetry, collected largely in the *Adi Granth* and scriptures of the Dadu Panth, invokes the names of fellow bhaktas like Kabir and Namdev, suggesting the proud sense of Bhakti fellowship that existed among the disadvantaged sections of society of the time.

Salabega was an Oriya Bhakti poet, born in the early seventeenth century. His father was a Mughal nobleman and his mother a Brahmin widow. When Salabega was wounded in battle, his mother instructed him to pray to Lord Jagannath of Puri. He did and was evidently healed—an event that turned him into a devout Vaishnavite. Although, as a Muslim, he was denied entry into the Puri temple, it is said that the ratha or chariot of Lord Jagannath actually paused on one occasion when he was away on a Vrindavan pilgrimage, and waited for him to return before continuing its yatra. The chariot pauses at his samadhi shrine to this very day, in honour of a poet who composed hundreds of well-loved devotional lyrics (with their signature couplets called *bhanita*) in praise of his beloved deity.

Sambandar (or Tirujnanasambandar) was a seventh-century poet, and an important figure among the sixty-three Nayanmar or Shaiva saints. His hymns to Shiva were collected to form the first three volumes of the *Tirumurai*, the twelve-volume canon of Tamil Shaiva devotional poetry. He is believed to have composed his first poem at the age of three when breast-fed by the goddess Parvati herself. He spent the rest of his short life as a wandering minstrel, worshipping at Shiva shrines all over Tamil Nadu. He is believed to have played a major role in re-establishing the Shaiva faith, and checking the expansion of the Jaina and Buddhist movements. According to legend, he attained liberation at the age of sixteen on the day of his wedding.

Sami (1743–1850) was an important figure in Sindhi Bhakti literature and the last of what has come to be known as the Trinity of the Golden Age of Sindhi poetry, alongside the Sufi poets Shah Abdul Latif and Sachal Sarmast. Although his name was Bhai Chainrai Bachomal Dataramani, he seems to have taken on the name Sami after his meeting with his master or 'real friend', Sami Meghraj. Translator Menka Shivdasani has written of his unique habit of writing his verse on slips of paper and storing them in earthen pitchers. His poetry, *Sami Ja Shlok*, reveals the influence of Vedantic as well as Sufi thought and Sanskrit poetic traditions.

Sankaradeva (1449–1568) was an Assamese polymath: mystic, poet, scholar, playwright and religious and social reformer. He inspired the Bhakti movement in Assam, and his legacy of neo-Vaishnavism (*Eka Sarana Hari Nama Dharma*) and the Sattras or monastic institutions he established, continue to flourish as living traditions even today. His literary output was prodigious, encompassing prose, verse, translations, compilations and doctrinal treatises in three languages: Assamese, Assamese Brajabuli and Sanskrit. He is credited with having devised new forms of music (*Borgeet*), theatrical performance (*Ankia Nat/ Bhaona*), Sattriya dance and a literary language (Assamese Brajabuli).

Soyarabai was a fourteenth-century Marathi woman saint-poet and a historic figure in the Varkari cult. She was also the wife of Chokhamela, a popular poet devoted to Lord Vithoba of Pandharpur. She belonged to the Mahar caste, historically identified as untouchable. In her sixty-odd extant abhangas, she asserts her love of Vithoba and denounces Brahmin orthodoxy and caste discrimination on the spiritual path with fiery eloquence. She is said to have made the annual pilgrimage to Pandharpur with her husband for several years.

Sundarar or Sundaramurti (the Handsome One), also known as Tampizhan Tozhan (Comrade of the Master), was a Shaiva poet during the eighth and ninth centuries, and an important figure in the sacred trio of saints in Tamil Shaivism, along with Appar and Sambandar. Born into a Brahmin family, he lived in Tiruvarur and like the other Nayanmar, travelled to other temples in Tamil Nadu to sing the praises of Shiva. He married twice, and his courtly life contrasts with the more austere lives of Appar and Sambandar. His devotional poems are collected in a work called the *Thiruthondathogai*. The seventh volume of the *Tirumurai*, the twelve-volume anthology of the poetry of Tamil Shaiva Siddhanta, comprises his poems. An unusual tone of friendship and familiarity with the Divine characterizes Sundarar's bhakti poetry. A celebrated poem by him begins by describing Shiva as 'pitta', madman.

Surdas was a sixteenth-century poet-saint, popularly believed to have been blind since birth. As the scholar John Hawley writes, 'By common consent, the poet regarded as the epitome of literary artistry in Brajbhasha is Surdas.' There are several popular legends about this contemporary of Mirabai, including tales of childhood deprivation, unsympathetic parents and congenital blindness (which may actually have been a figurative reference to spiritual condition rather than a physical one). His encounter with the great Vaishnava guru, Vallabhacharya, is believed to have had a lasting impact on his life, altering his approach to poetry and spirituality. Regarded as one of the foremost poets of Krishna, he left behind a considerable oeuvre of poems in a work called the *Sur Sagar*, which continue to be widely sung on concert stages even today.

Tukaram was a poet and mystic of the seventeenth century, and is one of the most influential poets in the Marathi language. He disappeared at the age of forty-one, leaving behind nearly 5000 poems or abhangas. A Shudra by birth, Tukaram wrote a colloquial Marathi verse in praise of Lord Vitthal (Vishnu)—his choice of language and his low caste constituting 'a double encroachment on brahmin monopoly', as his translator Dilip Chitre points out. The manuscript of his poems on display in the Vithoba temple in his native village, Dehu, is the same one that is believed to have miraculously surfaced, absolutely intact, thirteen days after orthodox Brahmins forced him to sink it in the local river Indrayani.

Tulsidas is one of India's best-known Bhakti poets. He lived in the sixteenth century, and spent most of his life in the city of Varanasi. Renowned for his devotion to Rama (and often considered an incarnation of Valmiki), his celebrated works are the *Ramcharitmanas*, his retelling of the Ramayana in the Avadhi dialect of medieval Hindi, and the *Vinaya Patrika* in Brajbhasha.

A supposed pivotal moment in his life was when, unable to contain his ardour, he is said to have swum across the river Yamuna by night and climbed up to his wife's bedroom when she was visiting her parental home. She chided him saying that if he were as devoted to Lord Rama as he was to her body, he would already have attained liberation. Chastened by the rebuke, he renounced the life of the householder, and devoted himself to a life of austerity and devotion.

Vatsara was a woman poet of the Varkari tradition of Maharashtra, who probably belonged to the Mahar caste. Little is known about her life.

Vidyapati (1352–1448) was a Maithili poet and Sanskrit writer of the fourteenth century whose work has been widely influential in the literary traditions of Eastern India. While he wrote poetry to Shiva as well, his love songs, which number more than 500, are in the lineage of Vaishnava Bhakti. Informed by his intimate knowledge of secular Sanskrit love poetry and of Jayadeva's *Gita Govinda*, these describe the love of Radha and Krishna, the metaphor of their physical union working on the level of the sensuous and spiritual all at once. Born in the Madhubani district of the Mithila region of modern-day Bihar, he was a well-known Sanskrit scholar and writer of his time, but it is his shift from Sanskrit to Maithili that made him a path-breaking figure in the history of a new literature.

Notes on Translators

Amit Chaudhuri is the author of five award-winning novels, two books of essays, a critical study, and a book of short stories. His sixth novel, *Odysseus Abroad*, is being published in the UK next year. He is Fellow of the Royal Society of Literature, and Professor of Contemporary Literature at the University of East Anglia. He is also an acclaimed musician who has performed all over the world.

Anand Thakore has written three collections of poetry: *Waking in December* (2001), *Elephant Bathing* (2012) and *Mughal Sequence* (2012). A Hindustani classical vocalist by profession, he trained for many years with Pandit Satyasheel Deshpande and has given concerts in various parts of the country. He is the founder of Harbour Line, a publishing collective, and runs Kshitij, an interactive forum for musicians. He lives in Mumbai where he teaches Hindustani vocal music.

A.K. Ramanujan (1929–1993) was a poet, translator, folklorist, philologist and Professor of Dravidian Studies at the University of Chicago. His translations include *Speaking of Siva*, and *Hymns for the Drowning*, selections from the *Tiruviruttam* and *Tiruvaymoli* of Nammalvar, and two collections of classical Tamil verse, *The Interior Landscape* (1967) and *Poems of Love and War* (1985). His poetry collections include *The Striders* (1966), *Relations* (1971), *Selected Poems* (1976), *Second Sight* (1986) and *Collected Poems* (1995). He received the Padma Shri in 1976.

Archana Venkatesan is Associate Professor of Comparative Literature and Religious Studies at the University of California, Davis. Her research interests are in the intersection of text and performance in South India, and the English translation of early and medieval Tamil poetry. She is the author of *The Secret Garland: Andal's Tiruppāvai and Nācciyār Tirumoḻi* (2010) and *A Hundred Measures of Time: The Tiruviruttam of Nammalvar*. She is presently collaborating with Francis Clooney on an English translation of Nammalvar's *Tiruvāymoḻi*.

Arvind Krishna Mehrotra is the editor of *The Oxford India Anthology of Twelve Modern Indian Poets* (1992)*, Collected Poems in English* by Arun Kolatkar (2010), and *An Illustrated History of Indian Literature in English* (2003), and the translator of *The Absent Traveller: Prakrit Love Poetry* (2008) and *Songs of Kabir* (2011). His essays are collected in *Partial Recall: Essays on Literature and Literary History (*2012). His *Collected Poems 1969-2014* has been published recently.

Professor Amaresh Datta headed the Department of English, Guwahati University for a record period of two decades, first as a Reader till May 1963 and then as a Professor (January 1964–

February 1980). Professsor Amaresh Datta was a close associate of Professor Maheswar Neog.

Barbara Stoler Miller (1940–1993) was a scholar of Sanskrit, well-known for her translation of the *Bhagavad Gita* (which became highly popular in the US). She also translated several works of Sanskrit drama and poetry, including the works of Jayadeva (*Love Song of the Dark Lord: Jayadeva's Gitagovinda*), Bhartrihari, Bhilhana and Kalidasa. She became Head of Department of Asian and Middle Eastern Cultures at Barnard College in New York City in 1979.

B.K. Barua (1908–1964) was a scholar and litterateur from Assam. A pioneer in the study of North-eastern folklore in India, he was one of the many founders of Guwahati University. He has won acclaim for his contribution to Assamese letters as a novelist and literary critic.

David Shulman is Renee Lang Professor of Humanistic Studies at the Hebrew University of Jerusalem, Israel. He specializes in the languages, literatures, and religions of southern India, particularly the medieval period. His many publications include collaborations with Velcheru Narayana Rao, Sanjay Subrahmanyam and Don Handelman, and extensive translations from Tamil, Telugu, and Sanskrit. Recent works include a volume of Hebrew translations of Tamil Sangam poetry and a monograph on the history of the imagination in South India.

Deben Bhattacharya (1921–2001) was an ethnomusicologist, filmmaker, writer, photographer, and radio producer. He produced several influential field recordings of music in Bengal, over a hundred records and twenty-odd films, besides writing extensively on folk music, poetry and dance, and his travels through South and Central Asia. His books include *Songs of the Qawals of India, Songs of the Bards of Bengal* and *Love Songs of Vidyapati*. He divided his time between Kolkata and Europe.

Dilip Chitre (1938–2009) was a poet, translator, critic, editor, painter and documentary filmmaker. He wrote in both English and Marathi, and translated extensively from the Varkari tradition. His book of translations of Tukaram, *Says Tuka*, received wide acclaim. He authored several poetry collections, his last in English being *As Is, Where Is: Selected Poems* (2008).

Gieve Patel is a poet, playwright, painter and translator. He has written three books of poetry: *Poems* (1966); *How Do You Withstand, Body* (1976); and *Mirrored Mirroring* (1991). He is also the author of three plays and has held several exhibitions of his paintings in India and abroad. He has been working on his Akho translations for several decades. He lives in Mumbai.

H.S. Shivaprakash is a poet, playwright and translator from Karnataka. His translations and adaptations of Shakespeare have been widely staged. He has also translated several well-known European, Latin American and African poets into Kannada and leading Kannada and Tamil poets into English. A former editor of the journal *Indian Literature*, he is Professor, Theatre and Performance Studies, Jawaharlal Nehru University, New Delhi. He is presently Director, The Tagore Centre, in the Embassy of India, in Berlin.

Indira Viswanathan Peterson specializes in Sanskrit and Tamil literature, Hinduism, South Indian performing arts and cultural history. She is David B. Truman Professor of Asian Studies at Mount Holyoke College, Massachusetts. Her book, *Poems to Siva: The Hymns of the Tamil Saints*, a significant study and translation of Shaiva Bhakti poetry and its performance in South Indian temples, was published in 1989.

Jerry Pinto is a Mumbai-based poet. His *Asylum and Other Poems* was published in 2004. He has translated Sachin Kundalkar's *Cobalt Blue* from Marathi (2013) and is working on a translation of Daya Pawar's seminal autobiography, *Baluta*. He has edited Adil Jussawalla's *Maps for a Mortal Moon: Essays and Entertainments* (2014) and is the author of the award-winning novel, *Em and the Big Hoom* (2012).

John Stratton Hawley is Professor of Religion at Barnard College. He has written and edited sixteen books, mainly on Hinduism and the Bhakti tradition of North India. These include *Three Bhakti Voices: Mirabai, Surdas and Kabir in Their Times and Ours* and *The Memory of Love: Surdas Sings to Krishna*, among others. He has been a Guggenheim Fellow, received several awards and was recently elected to the American Academy of Arts and Sciences.

Keki N. Daruwalla, one of India's distinguished litterateurs, writes poetry and fiction and lives in Delhi. His latest volume of poetry, *Fire Altar: Poems on the Persians and the Greeks* has just been published. His novel, *For Pepper and Christ,* was shortlisted for the Commonwealth Prize for Asia–UK. He was a member of the Jury for the Montreal Poetry Prize.

Khushwant Singh (1915–2014) was a novelist, short fiction writer, journalist and columnist. He served as editor of several literary and news publications, including *The Illustrated Weekly of India* and *Hindustan Times*. Some of his major books include *Train to Pakistan* and *A History of the Sikhs*. His works ranged from political commentary and satire on current affairs to major translations of Sikh religious texts and Urdu poetry. He received the Padma Vibhushan in 2007.

Linda Hess is a scholar, writer and lover of Kabir. She is Senior Lecturer in the Department of Religious Studies at Stanford University and Co-Director of Stanford's Center for South Asia. She has been researching the oral traditions of Kabir in recent years.

Maheswar Neog (1915–1995) was a poet and scholar of Assamese literature and culture who authored numerous books on the subject. His book, *Sankardeva and His Times: Early History of the Vaishnava Faith and Movement in Assam*, is considered a landmark work. A professor at Guwahati University, he helped open up North-eastern cultural history to the rest of India and the world. He received the Padma Shri in 1974.

Mark Juergensmeyer is Director of the Orfalea Center for Global and International Studies, Professor of Sociology and Affiliate Professor of Religious Studies at the University of Califorina, Santa Barbara. He is an expert on religious violence, conflict resolution and South Asian religions and politics. He has published over two hundred articles and twenty books, including *Global Rebellion: Religious Challenges to the Secular State.*

Meena Desai has been translating Gujarati poetry since the 1980s, and retains a deep belief in translation as essential to human connection. Her doctoral research was about communication in drama. She worked in the telecommunications industry, and continues to devote herself to cross-cultural communication in various ways. She has translated several Gujarati *ghazal*s to share major contributions that remain relatively unknown. For over ten years she has worked on Narsinh Mehta's poetry for the same reason. She lives in the US.

Menka Shivdasani has authored two poetry collections, and is co-translator of an anthology of Sindhi Partition poetry. She has edited an anthology of poetry for www.bigbridge.org, and an anthology of women's writing for Sound and Picture Archives for Research on Women (SPARROW). She is the Founder–Member of Mumbai's Poetry Circle, the Mumbai Coordinator for 100 Thousand Poets for Change, and a Founding member of Asia Pacific Writers & Translators Association.

Mohan Gehani is a Sindhi poet, playwright, writer and critic. He has been associated with various literary organizations and publications for over fifty years. His research on the history of Sind and his book, *Brief Introduction: History of Sind*, are widely acclaimed. His collection of plays, *Ta Khawban Jo Cha Thindo . . .* (What will Happen to Our Dreams), won the Sahitya Akademi award in 2011.

Mustansir Dalvi teaches architecture, and is a poet and translator. His English translation of Muhammad Iqbal's work from the Urdu, *Taking Issue and Allah's Answer* (2012), is described as 'insolent and heretical'. This book was Runner-Up for Best Translation for 2012 at the Muse India National Literary Awards. His book of poems, *brouhahas of cocks*, was published in 2013, and his translations of Marathi poet Hemant Divate, *struggles with imagined gods,* in 2014.

Neela Bhagwat is a classical khayal singer of the Gwalior gharana. She holds Master's degrees in Marathi, Sanskrit and Sociology, and attempts to interpret medieval saint-poetry in the contemporary context and in humanitarian terms. Disturbed by the communal violence in Mumbai (1992–93) and Gujarat (2002), she chooses to sing the poetry of peace and love of Kabir, Mirabai, Tukaram, Chokhamela, Muktabai, Soyarabai, Janabai, Nirmala, Kanhopatra, and other Bhakti mystics.

Norman Cutler (1949–2002) was a scholar of Tamil literary history and Bhakti poetry, influential in presenting Tamil as a classical language to the Western world. *Songs of Experience: The Poetics of Tamil Devotion* was the title of his significant work on Tamil religious poetry. He was Chairman of the South Asian Languages and Civilizations Department at the University of Chicago where he spent his entire career.

Prabhanjan K. Mishra lives in Mumbai. He loves reading, writing and translating poetry and fiction across two languages: Oriya and English. He is a seeker, curious about both mysticism and physics. His poems in English are collected in three books: *Vigil, Lips of a Canyon* and *Litmus*. His poetry and short fiction have been widely anthologized and published in various journals. He has been President of Mumbai's Poetry Circle.

Priya Sarukkai Chabria is a poet, novelist, essayist and translator with five published books. Her work has been translated into six languages, and published in journals, websites and anthologies. She is the recipient of the Outstanding Contribution to Literature award from the Indian Government. Miniature painting and cinema are her other passions. Forthcoming in 2015 are translations of the Tamil mystic poet Andal, with poet Ravi Shankar, and a short-story collection. She edits Poetry at Sangam (www.sangamhouse.org). For more information, please visit www.priyawriting.com

Ravi Shankar is founding editor of Drunken Boat and author/editor of eight books and chapbooks of poetry, including *Deepening Groove*, winner of the 2010 National Poetry Review Prize, and W.W. Norton's *Language for a New Century: Contemporary Poetry from Asia, the Middle East and Beyond*. He has appeared in *The New York Times* and the BBC, won a Pushcart Prize, and teaches at CCSU and in the Master of Fine Arts Program at City University of Hong Kong.

Rahul Soni is a writer, editor and translator. He has edited *Home from a Distance* (2011), an anthology of Hindi poetry in English translation, and translated *Magadh* (2013), a collection of poems by Shrikant Verma, and *The Roof Beneath Their Feet* (2013), a novel by Geetanjali Shree.

Ranjit Hoskote is a poet, cultural theorist and curator. His collections of poetry include *Vanishing Acts: New and Selected Poems 1985-2005* (2006) and *Central Time* (2014). His translation of the fourteenth-century Kashmiri mystic Lal Ded has appeared as *I,*

Lalla: The Poems of Lal Ded (2011). A long-time student of the Yogachara Buddhist and Kashmir Shaivite traditions, Hoskote applies their accounts of consciousness, temporality, memory and subjectivity to the urgencies of contemporary culture.

Sampurna Chattarji is a poet, novelist and translator. Her works of poetry include *Sight May Strike You Blind* (2007) and *Absent Muses* (2010); her two novels are *Rupture* (2009) and *Land of the Well* (2012). *Dirty Love* (2013) is her short-story collection about Bombay/Mumbai. *Wordygurdyboom!* (2004, 2008) is Sampurna's translation of Sukumar Ray's Bengali poetry and prose; and *Selected Poems* (2014), her translation of the Bengali poet Joy Goswami. For more information, please visit http://sampurnachattarji.wordpress.com

Shukdev Singh is an author and translator. He retired as a Professor at Banaras Hindu University.

Velcheru Narayana Rao is currently Distinguished Visiting Professor at Emory University, Atalanta, GA, USA. Earlier he served as Krishnadevaraya Professor of Languages and Cultures of Asia, University of Wisconsin-Madison, USA. His publications include *Srinatha: The Poet who Made Gods and Kings* (with David Shulman) and *Textures of Time: Writing History in South India 1600-1800* (with David Shulman and Sanjay Subrahmanyam).

Vijay Nambisan is a poet, prose writer and translator. His works of poetry include *Gemini* (1992) and *First Infinities* (2014). As prose writer, he is the author of *Bihar is in the Eye of the Beholder* (2000). His essay, 'Language as an Ethic', was published in 2003.

As translator, he is the author of *Two Measures of Bhakti: Puntanam and Melpattur* (2009).

Vinay Dharwadker, Professor of Comparative Literature, University of Wisconsin–Madison, translates from Hindi, Marathi, Urdu, Punjabi, and Sanskrit. His collection of poetry is titled *Sunday at the Lodi Gardens* (1994). He has edited *The Oxford Anthology of Modern Indian Poetry* (1994), *The Collected Essays of A.K. Ramanujan* (1999) and *The Norton Anthology of World Literature* (2012) and translated *Kabir: The Weaver's Songs* (2003) for Penguin Classics. Forthcoming translations include Mohan Rakesh's *One Day in the Season of Rain* and Kalidasa's *Shakuntala*.

Sources

PUBLISHED

Akka Mahadevi

Speaking of Siva, translated by A.K. Ramanujan, Penguin Books India, 1973.

I Keep Vigil of Rudra: The Vachanas, translated by H.S. Shivaprakash, Penguin Books India, 2010.

Allama Prabhu

Speaking of Siva, translated by A.K. Ramanujan, Penguin Books India, 1973.

I Keep Vigil of Rudra: The Vachanas, translated by H.S. Shivaprakash, Penguin Books India, 2010.

Andal

The Secret Garland: Translations of Andal's Tiruppāvai and *Nācciyār Tirumoḻi,* translated by Archana Venkatesan, Oxford University Press, 2009.

Priya Sarukkai Chabria; *Nachiyar Tirumoli*, Verse One; Tai oru tinkal; first published in *Post Road*, Number 22 (Boston University Journal of Literature), Spring 2011. www.postroadmag.com/22/index.phtml.

Ravi Shankar; first published in *Post Road*, Number 22 (Boston University Journal of Literature), Spring 2011. www.postroadmag.com/22/index.phtml.

Annamacharya

God on the Hill: Temple Poems from Tirupati: Annamayya, translated by V. Narayana Rao and David Shulman, Oxford University Press, 2005.

Appar

Poems to Shiva: The Hymns of the Tamil Saints, translated by Indira Viswanathan Peterson, Motilal Banarsidass Publishers Pvt. Ltd, 2007.

Basavanna

Speaking of Siva, translated by A.K. Ramanujan, Penguin Books India, 1973.

I Keep Vigil of Rudra: The Vachanas, translated by H.S. Shivaprakash, Penguin Books India, 2010.

Chandidas

Love Songs of Chandidas: The Rebel Poet-Priest of Bengal, translated by Deben Bhattacharya, Grove Press, 1970.

Chowdaiah

I Keep Vigil of Rudra: The Vachanas, translated by H.S. Shivaprakash, Penguin Books India, 2010.

Devara Dasimayya

Speaking of Siva, translated by A.K. Ramanujan, Penguin Books India, 1973.

I Keep Vigil of Rudra: The Vachanas, translated by H.S. Shivaprakash, Penguin Books India, 2010.

Dhoolaiah

I Keep Vigil of Rudra: The Vachanas, translated by H.S. Shivaprakash, Penguin Books India, 2010.

Gangambike

I Keep Vigil of Rudra: The Vachanas, translated by H.S. Shivaprakash, Penguin Books India, 2010.

Janabai

'Jana sweeps with a broom' and 'Jani loosens her hair' from unpublished manuscript, 2008, *Poets of Vithoba* by Dilip Chitre; Poetrywala, 2014 (forthcoming); first published in *The Oxford Anthology of Bhakti Literature*, edited by Andrew Schelling, Oxford University Press, 2011.

Jayadeva

The Gitagovinda of Jayadeva: Love Song of the Dark Lord, translated by Barbara Stoler Miller. Motilal Banarsidass, Columbia University Press, 1977 (20th anniversary edition).

Jnaneshwar

'Blue is this sky' from unpublished manuscript, 2008, *Poets of Vithoba* by Dilip Chitre; Poetrywala, 2014 (forthcoming); first published in

The Oxford Anthology of Bhakti Literature, edited by Andrew Schelling, Oxford University Press, 2011.

Kabir

Songs of Kabir, translated by Arvind Krishna Mehrotra, Everyman series, Hachette Book Publishing India with Black Kite/Permanent Black, 2011.

Bijak of Kabir, translated by Linda Hess and Shukdev Singh, Motilal Banarsidass Publishers Pvt. Ltd, 1986.

The Weaver's Song: Kabir, translated by Vinay Dharwadker, Penguin Books India, 2003.

Karaikkal Ammaiyar

Songs of Experience: The Poetics of Tamil Devotion, translated by Norman Cutler, Indiana University Press, 1987.

Kshetrayya

When God is a Customer: Telugu Courtesan Songs by Ksetrayya and Others, edited and translated by A.K. Ramanujan, Velcheru Narayana Rao and David Shulman, University of California Press, Berkeley, 1994.

Lal Ded

I Lalla: The Poems of Lal Ded, translated by Ranjit Hoskote, Penguin Books India, 2011.

Manikkavacakar

Hymns for the Drowning: Poems for Visnu by Nammalvar, translated from Tamil by A.K. Ramanujan, Penguin Books, 1993.

Nammalvar

Hymns for the Drowning: Poems for Visnu by Nammalvar, translated from Tamil by A.K. Ramanujan, Penguin Books, 1993.

Guru Nanak

Bara Maha, 'Magh' (January-February); 'Phalgun' (February-March); 'Chet' (March-April); 'Asan' (September-October).

The Japji and The Rehras, Verses 5 and 32, 'Japji', The Morning Prayer, translated by Khushwant Singh, Rupa Publications.

'Hymns of Guru Nanak, Songs of the Gurus: From Nanak to Gobind Singh', 'Numerous worlds', translated by Khushwant Singh; Penguin Viking, 2008.

Puntanam Namboodiri

Two Measures of Bhakti: Puntanam and Melpattur, translated by Vijay Nambisan, Penguin Classics, 2009.

Ravidas

Songs of the Saints, translated and edited by John Stratton Hawley and Mark Juergensmeyer, Oxford University Press, 1988.

Sambandar

Poems to Shiva: The Hymns of the Tamil Saints, translated by Indira Viswanathan Peterson, Motilal Banarsidass Publishers Pvt. Ltd, 2007.

Sankardeva

Renderings of Sankardeva by B.K. Barua and Maheswar Neog

Poetry, Religion and Culture: The Indian Perspective and Sankaradeva, translated by Amaresh Datta, www.atributetosankaradeva.org.

Sundarar

Poems to Shiva: The Hymns of the Tamil Saints, translated by Indira Viswanathan Peterson, Motilal Banarsidass Publishers Pvt. Ltd, 2007.

Surdas

Songs of the Saints of India, translated and edited by John Stratton Hawley and Mark Juergensmeyer, Oxford University Press, 1988.

Tukaram

Says Tuka: Selected Poetry of Tukaram, translated from the Marathi and with an Introduction by Dilip Chitre, Penguin Books, 1991.

Vidyapati
Love Songs of Vidyapati: Deben Bhattacharya, (ed.) W.G. Archer, Grove Press, 1970.

UNPUBLISHED

Abhirami Bhattar

aanandamaai en arivaai, nirainda amudamumaai (No. 11, Abhirami Antadi):
'Origin of rapture, wellspring of wisdom'
tanga shilai kondu, daanavar muppuram shaaittu (No. 62, Abhirami Antadi):
'He used the golden bow of Mount Meru'
*kurambai aduttu kudipukka aavi,veng kootrukkitta (*No. 49, Abhirami

Antadi):

'And one day death shall arrive'

virumbit tozhum adiyaar vizhineer malgi (No. 94, Abhirami Antadi):

'Their eyes deluged in ecstasy'

andre taduttenai aandukondaai kondadalla enkai (No. 30, Abhirami Antadi):

'And then you drenched me with your grace'

chinnanchiriya marungil shaattiya sheyya pattum (No. 53, Abhirami Antadi*):*

'Your waist slender'

nagaiye ikdinda nyaalam ellaam petra naayagikku (No. 93, Abhirami Antadi):

'Isn't it funny that though she's Mother of the Universe'

From *Abhirami Andadi* (English translation by Saundarya Rajesh), Giri Trading Agency Pvt. Ltd, Mumbai/ Chennai, 2011.

Project Madurai: www.projectmadurai.org/pm_etexts/pdf/ pm0026_01.pdf.

Akho

'Age and Decrepitude'; 'The Dude'; 'Turban tilted rakishly'; 'Where the creature is'; 'Fire! Fire! The town is in flames' from ———, / Akho.

Based on handwritten texts of Akho, given to Gieve Patel by Gujarati litterateur Suresh Joshi in the 1960s. Joshi did not indicate the source at the time.

Bahinabai

Vaate utho naye jeev zhaav tari: 'Such happiness then, such happiness'

From *Navaneet*, (ed.) Anant Kaakbaa Priyolkar, Mumbai Raajya Shikashan Khate Prakashan, 1957. First edition (ed.) Parshuram Ballal Godbole, 1854; second edition (ed.) Raoji Shastri Godbole, 1882; *Shri Sakal Santavaani*, vols 1 and 2, Gita Press, Gorakhpur.

Chokhamela

'Lord of the forsaken'

From *Poets of Vithoba*, by Dilip Chitre; unpublished manuscript, 2008, Poetrywala, 2014 (forthcoming).

Janabai

Doicha padar aalaa khaandyaavari: 'I have let my veil drop to my shoulders'

From *Navaneet*, (ed.) Anant Kaakbaa Priyolkar, Mumbai Raajya Shikashan Khate Prakashan, 1957. First edition (ed.) Parshuram Ballal Godbole, 1854; second edition (ed.) Raoji Shastri Godbole, 1882; *Shri Sakal Santavaani*, vols 1 and 2, Gita Press, Gorakhpur.

Kanhopatra

Patit paavan mhanavisi aadhi: 'We're told you're the holiest of holies'

From *Navaneet* (ed.) Anant Kaakbaa Priyolkar, Mumbai Raajya Shikashan Khate Prakashan, 1957. First edition (ed.) Parshuram Ballal Godbole, 1854; second edition (ed.) Raoji Shastri Godbole, 1882; *Shri Sakal Santavaani*, vols 1 and 2, Gita Press, Gorakhpur.

Lalon Fakir

Chand dhoraphandjanona re mon: 'Mind, you don't know the gag'
Hiralal Motir dokaanegelena: 'Hiralal, you never went to Moti's shop'

From *Ramprasadi* (ed.), Sarbananda Chaudhuri, Sahitya Akademi, New Delhi, 2007.

Mirabai

Matwaro badar aaye re, hari ko saneso kachhu na laye re: 'Drunken clouds'
Rana mahne ya badnami lage meethi: 'Rana, this shame is so sweet'
Mayeri maha liya govinda mol: 'Friend, I went and bought Govind'
Pag baandh ghungriyo nachiyari: 'I dance wearing ankle bells'
Papiyare piv ki vani na bol: 'Feverbird stop crying'
Mhara ri girdhar gopal doosra na koi: 'Only Giridhar is mine'
Nain to girdhar ke ghar jaoon: 'I'll go to Giridhar's home'

From *Maru Mandakini Meera*, edited and with an Introduction by Ratanlal Mishra, Jaipur: Sahityagar, 2010.

Muktabai

Deoolaanchi devo gharbari bhaavo: 'I sense him here. My God. From the temple. Here'
Mungdi udaali aakaashi: 'An ant flew into the sky'

From *Navaneet*, (ed.) Anant Kaakbaa Priyolkar, Mumbai Raajya Shikashan Khate Prakashan, 1957. First edition (ed.) Parshuram Ballal Godbole, 1854; second edition (ed.) Raoji Shastri Godbole, 1882; *Shri Sakal Santavaani*, vols 1 and 2, Gita Press, Gorakhpur.

Namdev

'Good that we've found out what makes you Almighty' and 'Tell me, O God, why you and I are cast in the roles of enemy'

From *Poets of Vithoba*, by Dilip Chitre; unpublished manuscript, 2008, Poetrywala, 2014 (forthcoming).

Narsinh Mehta

Palang Paaye Tane Kusum-mala Vade: 'To the foot of the bed I'll fasten your arms'
Sundariratna-Mukhachandra Avilokava: 'Transfixed on beauty's gem-like face'
Vichitra Ras Ne Navali Leela: 'Strange ecstasy and joy unique'
Giri Talaati Ane Kund Damodar: 'At the foot of the mountain is Damodar Pond'

From *Narasimha Mahetan Kavyakritio*, (ed.) Shivlal Jesalpura, Ahmedabad: Sahitya Sanshodhan Prakashan, 1981.

Nivruttinath

'The Greatness of Pandharpur' from *Poets of Vithoba*, by Dilip Chitre; unpublished manuscript, 2008, Poetrywala, 2014 (forthcoming).

Rahim

Jhoomi jhoomi chahoon ore barsat meghaa: 'All around us, clouds burst'
Aao, Sudhaakar pyare, neh nichod: 'This songbird craves'
http://blog.eaglespace.com/rahim-radha-krishna/ accessed on 4th May 2014.

Hari Rahim aisi kari, jyon kamaan sar poor: 'Well Rahim, what was Hari thinking'
Jaal pade jal jaat bahi taaji minan ko moh: 'Water soon drains away'
Je sulge te bujh gaye, bujhe te sulge naahi: 'That which smoulders, burns itself out'
Ab Rahim muskil padi, gaadhe dou kaam: 'Here is a fine fix, Rahim'
Raam na jaate harin sang, Siya na Raavan saath: 'What if Ram had not chased the deer'
http://pearlsofspirituality.wordpress.com/2011/07/20/rahim-ke-dohe/ accessed on 4th May 2014.

Jo baden ko laghu kahe, nahi Rahim ghati jaahi: 'Just calling a large thing small, Rahim'
www.geeta-kavita.com/hindi_sahitya.asp?id=440 accessed on 4th May 2014.

Rahiman gali hai saankri, dujo naahi thahraahi: 'The alley is narrow, Rahim'

From K.L. Vyas, in 'Rahim', from *Poet Saints of India*. Edited by M. Sivaramakrishna and Sumita Roy, New Delhi: Sterling Paperbacks, 1998.

Rajai

Ghardhyaani kela guru: 'The man of the house says he's found a guru'

From *Navaneet*, (ed.) Anant Kaakbaa Priyolkar, Mumbai Raajya Shikashan Khate Prakashan, 1957. First edition (ed.) Parshuram Ballal Godbole, 1854; second edition (ed.) Raoji Shastri Godbole, 1882; *Shri Sakal Santavaani*, vols 1 and 2, Gita Press, Gorakhpur.

Ramprasad Sen

Song 98: *Ramprasadi*: 'I won't be wheedled if you wheedle me again, my dear' [*Samvadprabhakar*, 13 March, 1855]
Song 56: *Ramprasadi*: 'Ma, who can comprehend your compassion' [*Prasad Prasanga*, pg. 100-101]
Song 69: *Ramprasadi*: 'Mind, you never lost this delusion' [*Prasad Prasanga*, pg. 65]
Song 48: *Ramprasadi*: 'Just try getting past me, Ma' [*Prasad Prasanga*, pg. 47]

From *Ramprasadi*, (ed.) Sarbananda Chaudhuri, Sahitya Akademi, New Delhi, 2007.

Salabega

Bagha Matilare Nikunja Vanara: 'Out of his desolate jungle cave, a panther's on the prowl'
Eka Mo Bhakata-Jivana: 'In my devotees' love, I build my home'
Jaa Jaa Mo Tharu Tumbhe Rasika Kanhai: 'Get lost, you dirty flirt'

From *Bhaktakabi Salabega (Jibani O Padyabali),* compiled by Pandit Nilamani Mishra, Cuttack: Grantha Mandira, Binodbihari, 5th edition.

Sami

Prem Akhru Padhe, Satguru Mana Sital Kayo: 'The word 'love' taught by my Sadguru'
Aayo Nagar Natu bekh daare bazar mein: 'The actor Nagar has come in disguise'

Soee Saudagar, khep khati ghar aayo: 'He is a true trader who has brought riches home'
Prem pravah wahiyo waee budh budhi kare: 'In a torrent of love, reason drowned'

From *Sami ja Shlok*, compiled by Prof. B.H. Nagrani; reissued by Sindhi Academy, Delhi, 1997.

Soyarabai

Kiti kiti bolo deva: 'How much more must I plead, Lord?'
Dehaasi vitaal mhanti sakal: 'You say some bodies are untouchable'
Avgha rang ek zhaala: 'One colour now, one colour, you and me'

From *Navaneet*, (ed.) Anant Kaakbaa Priyolkar, Mumbai Raajya Shikashan Khate Prakashan, 1957. First edition (ed.) Parshuram Ballal Godbole, 1854; second edition (ed.) Raoji Shastri Godbole, 1882; *Shri Sakal Santavaani*, vols 1 and 2, Gita Press, Gorakhpur.

Surdas

adhar saji balbeer: 'The flute has but to touch his lips'

From *Sursagar*. Surdas bhajan.

Tulsidas

Abalao nasani ab na nasaiho: 'I have wasted much time'

From *Vinaypatrika*, Tulsidas bhajan, *Tulsi Ek Darshan*, Pandit Kumar Gandharva, Live concert recording.

'The name of Rama'

Doha from the *Adikanda* in the *Ramacharitmanas*, Adikanda, Gita Press, Gorakhpur.

Vatsara

Sharir vikle charnaasi: 'My head? Sold to your feet'

From Navaneet, (ed.) Anant Kaakbaa Priyolkar, Mumbai Raajya Shikashan Khate Prakashan, 1957. First edition (ed.) Parshuram Ballal Godbole, 1854; second edition (ed.) Raoji Shastri Godbole, 1882; *Shri Sakal Santavaani*, vols 1 and 2, Gita Press, Gorakhpur.

Copyright Acknowledgements

Every effort has been made to trace copyright holders and obtain permission. Any omissions brought to our attention will be remedied in future editions.

A.K. Ramanujan: The estate of A.K. Ramanujan and Krishna Ramanujan for translations 'Don't you take on this thing'; 'Don't make me hear all day'; 'The rich will make'; 'Cripple me father'; 'They plunge wherever they see water'; 'I am no worshipper'; 'When like a hailstone'/Basavanna; 'Better than meeting'; 'Like an elephant'; 'You are the forest'; 'People, male and female'; 'What's to come tomorrow'; 'I love the handsome one'; 'I have Maya for mother-in-law'; 'Like a silkworm weaving her house'/Akka Mahadevi; 'Whatever it was'; 'I am the one who has the body'; 'God of my clan'; 'If they see'/Dasimayya; 'Looking for your light'; 'The wind sleeps'; 'With a whole temple'/Allama Prabhu; 'He grabbed me'/Manikkavacakar from *Speaking of Siva*, translated by A.K. Ramanujan, Penguin Books India, 1973.

——— for translations 'You dwell in Heaven'; 'Before I could say a million'; 'We here and that man, this man'; 'The Lord at play'; 'My Lord, my Cannibal'; 'The Takeover'; 'The Playboy' from *Hymns for the Drowning: Poems for Visnu by Nammalvar*, translated from Tamil by A.K. Ramanujan, Penguin Books India, 1993.

A.K. Ramanujan, Velcheru Narayana Rao and David Shulman: For 'A woman to her reluctant lover'/Kshetrayya in *When God is a Customer: Telugu Courtesan Songs by Ksetrayya and Others by* A.K. Ramanujan, Velcheru Narayana Rao, and David Shulman, University of California, © 1994 by the Regents of the University of California.

Amaresh Datta: for translation 'What have you done, O Gopala'/ Sankaradeva.

Amit Chaudhuri: for translation 'It's ages since I saw you'/ Chandidas.

Anand Thakore: for translations 'The name of Rama'/ *Ramacharitmanas*; 'I have wasted much time' (*Abalao nasani ab na nasaiho*)/Tulsidas; 'The flute has but to touch his lips and see' (*adhar saji balbeer*)/Surdas.

Archana Venkatesan: for translations 'I lie here yearning for the familiar sight'; 'I melt. I fray, But he does not care'/Andal from *The Secret Garland: Translations of Andal's Tiruppavai* and *Nacciyar Tirumoli*, translated by Archana Venkatesan, Oxford University Press, 2009.

——— 'Some send their heart'; 'The texts of philosophy may speak'/Nammalvar from *A Hundred Measures of Time*, *Tiruviruttam* by Nammalvar, translated by Archana Venkatesan, Penguin Books India, 2014.

Arundhathi Subramaniam: for translations 'Origin of rapture, wellspring of wisdom' (*aanandamaai en arivaai, nirainda amudamumaai*); 'He used the golden bow of Mount Meru' (*tanga shilai kondu, daanavar muppuram shaaittu*); 'And one day death shall arrive' (*kurambai aduttu kudipukka aavi,veng kootrukkitta*); 'Their eyes deluged in ecstasy' (*virumbit tozhum adiyaar vizhineer malgi*); 'And then you drenched me with your grace' (*andre taduttenai aandukondaai kondadalla enkai*); 'Your waist slender' (*chinnanchiriya marungil shaattiya sheyya pattum*); 'Isn't it funny that though she's Mother of the Universe' (*nagaiye ikdinda nyaalam ellaam petra naayagikku*)/ Abhirami Bhattar.

Arvind Krishna Mehrotra: for translations 'Like a sharp arrow'; 'Death has them in its sights'; 'I beat on your door'; 'Listen carefully'; 'O pandit, your hair-splitting's'; ' While you are busy perfuming'; 'If we're still strangers'; 'Chewing slowly'; 'The yogi's a solitary'; 'Think twice before you keep'; 'Brother I've seen some astonishing sights'; 'What is this untellable tale about'; 'I won't come' from *Songs of Kabir*, translated by Arvind Krishna Mehrotra, Everyman series, Hachette Book Publishing India with Black Kite/Permanent Black, 2011.

Barbara Stoler Miller: Columbia University Press for translations 'The Ninth Song' and 'The Tenth Song' from *The Gita Govinda of Jayadeva: Love Song of the Dark Lord*; Barbara Stoler Miller, Columbia University Press, 1977 (20th anniversary edition). Reprinted with permission from the publisher.

B.K. Barua and Maheswar Neog: for translation 'He is my master'/Sankaradeva.

Deben Bhattacharya: Grove Press and Deben Bhattacharya for translations 'The essence of beauty'; 'She lingers out of doors'; 'I throw ashes at all laws'/Chandidas from *Love Songs of Chandidas: The Rebel Poet-Priest of Bengal* (New York: Grove Press).

———— 'O Friend I cannot tell you'; 'He left me saying he would be back tomorrow'; 'How the rain falls'; 'Seeing the bright moon'/ Vidyapati from *Love Songs of Vidyapati*: Deben Bhattacharya, 1970; Edited by W.G. Archer, Grove Press, New York.

Dilip Chitre: Vijaya Chitre for translations 'The Great Ghost of Pandhari'; 'Who is the one'; 'I cannot bear the day'; 'The whole

a lamp'; 'I fritter away my life in lies'; 'In everlasting bondage to you'; 'O madman, with the moon-crowned hair'; 'I have praised you, saying all I can say'/Sundarar; 'Simple parrot'; 'Tiruvayaru is the place'/Sambandar; 'In vain I pampered the body'; 'Why chant the Veda?'; 'Why rise at dawn and bathe'; 'I who only cared for my pride'; 'Once a slave of past karma'; 'When I board the boat of my mind'; 'Plow the field with true faith'/Appar from *Poems to Shiva: The Hymns of the Tamil Saints*, translated by Indira Viswanath Peterson, Motilal Banarsidass Publishers Pvt. Ltd, 2007.

Jerry Pinto and Neela Bhagwat: for translations 'How much more must I plead' (*Kiti kiti bolo deva*); 'You say some bodies are untouchable' (*Dehaasi vitaal mhanti sakal*); 'One colour now, one colour, you and me' (*Avgha rang ek zhaala*)/Soyarabai; 'We're told you're the holiest of holies' (*Patit paavan mhanavisi aadhi*); Kanhopatra; 'I have let her veil drop' (*Doicha padar aalaa khaandyaavari*)/Janabai; 'The Man of the House' (*Ghardhyaani kela guru*)/Rajai; 'I sense him here' (*Deoolaanchi Devo Gharbari Bhaavo*); 'An ant flew into the sky' (*Mungdi udaali aakaashi*)/Muktabai; 'Such happiness then, such happiness' (*Vaate utho naye jeev zhaav tari*)/Bahinabai; 'My head? Sold to your feet' (*Sharir vikle charnaasi*)/Vatsara.

John Stratton Hawley and Mark Jurgensmeyer: for translations 'The walls are made of water'; 'It's just a clay puppet'; 'The regal realm with the sorrowless name'; 'I've never known how to tan or sew'/Ravidas; 'Unless you wake up to what you are'; 'She's found him, she has'; 'Radha is lost to the onslaught of love'; 'I, only I, am the best at being worst'; 'Gopal has slipped in and stolen my heart'; 'Ever since your name has entered Hari's ear'; 'Life has stumbled, stumbled, unraveled'/Surdas from *Songs of the Saints*, translated and edited by John Stratton Hawley and Mark Jurgensmeyer, Oxford University Press, 1988.

Keki Daruwalla and Meena Desai: for translations 'At the foot of the mountain' (*Giri Talaati Ane Kund Damodar*); 'To the foot of the bed' (*Palang Paaye Tane Kusum-mala Vade*); 'Strange ecstasy and joy unique' (*Vichitra Ras Ne Navali Leela*); 'Transfixed on beauty' (*Sundariratna-Mukhachandra Avilokava*)/Narsinh Mehta.

Khushwant Singh: Mala Dayal for translations 'It is the month of Chet'; 'O Master, come to me'; 'The Lord has entered my being'/ Magh; 'She whose heart is full of love'/Nanak from *Bara Masa*.

———— 'He cannot be proved for he is uncreated'; 'Were I given a thousand tongues'/Nanak from *The Japji and The Rehras*, translated by Khushwant Singh, Rupa Publications.

———— 'Numerous worlds'/Nanak from *Songs of the Gurus: From Nanak to Gobind Singh,* translated by Khushwant Singh, Penguin Viking, 2008.

Linda Hess and Shukhdev Singh: for translations 'They searched and searched'; 'Lord a fire is raging'; 'Pandit do some research'; 'Death is standing on your head'; 'Grasp the root'; 'When the snake of separation'; 'This is the big fight, King Ram'; 'In the garden the bee lingers'; 'If I say one, it isn't so'/Kabir from *Bijak of Kabir*, translated by Linda Hess and Shukdev Singh, Motilal Banarsidass Publishers Pvt. Ltd, 1986.

Mohan Gehani and Menka Shivdasani: for translations 'That actor Nagar' (*Aayo Nagar Natu bekh daare bazar mein*); 'He who is a true trader' (*Soee Saudagar, khep khati ghar aayo*); 'In a torrent of love' (*Prem Pravah Wahiyo waee Budh Budhi Kare*); 'The word love' (*Prem Akhru Padhe, Satguru Mana Sital Kayo*)/Sami.

Mustansir Dalvi: for translations 'All around us' (*Jhoomi jhoomi chahoon ore barsat meghaa*); 'What if Ram hadn't chased the deer' (*Raam na jaate harin sang, Siya na Raavan saath*); 'The alley is narrow' (*Rahiman gali hai saankri, dujo naahi thahraahi*); 'This songbird craves but a glimpse of you' (*Aao, Sudhaakar pyare, neh nichod*); 'Water soon drains away' (*Jaal pade jal jaat bahi taaji minan ko moh*); 'Well Rahim, what was Hari thinking' (*Hari Rahim aisi kari, jyon kamaan sar poor*); 'Just calling a large thing small' (*Jo baden ko laghu kahe, nahi Rahim ghati jaahi*); 'That which smoulders burns itself out' (*Je sulge te bujh gaye, bujhe te sulge naahi*); 'Here is a fine fix' (*Ab Rahim muskil padi, gaadhe dou kaam*)/Rahim.

Norman Cutler: Indiana University Press for translation 'I became your slave'(Verse 61, Karaikkal Ammaiyar, *Arputatiruvandadi*) from *Songs of Experience: The Poetics of Tamil Devotion*, translated by Norman Cutler, Indiana University Press, 1987. Reprinted with permission of Indiana University Press.

Prabhanjan Mishra: for translations 'Get lost, you dirty flirt' (*Jaa Jaa Mo Tharu Tumbhe Rasika Kanhai*); 'In my devotees' love' (*Eka Mo Bhakata-Jivana*); 'Out of this desolate jungle cave' (*Bagha Matilare Nikunja Vanara*)/Salabega.

Priya Sarukkai Chabria: for translation 'With white hoops on moist sand' (*Nachiyar Tirumoli*, Verse One; *Tai oru tinkal*)/Andal.

Rahul Soni: for translations 'Drunken clouds'(*Matwaro badar aaye re, hari ko saneso kachhu na laye re*); 'Rana, this shame is so sweet'(*Rana mahne ya badnami lage meethi*); 'Friend, I went and bought Govind' (*Mayeri maha liya govinda mol*); 'I dance wearing ankle bells' (*Pag baandh ghungriyo nachiyari*); 'Fever-bird stop crying' (*Papiyare piv ki vani na bol*); 'Only Giridhar is mine' (*Mhara ri girdhar gopal doosra na koi*); 'I'll go to Giridhar's home'; (*Main to giridhar ke ghar jaoon*)/Mirabai.

Ranjit Hoskote: for translations 'Restless mind; This body that you are fussing'; 'Up woman! Go make your offering'; 'Lord! I've never known who I really am'; 'Some, who have closed their eyes'; 'I hacked my way through six forests'; 'I pestled my heart in love's mortar'; 'I am towing my boat'; 'Wisest to play the fool'; 'A thousand times at least'; 'Whatever my hands did was worship'; 'He laughs when you laugh'; 'Wrapped up in yourself'; 'I wore myself out'; 'I, Lalla, came through the gate of'; 'He knows the crown is the temple of Self'; 'Onion and garlic are one, I've learnt' from *I Lalla: The Poems of Lal Ded*, translated by Ranjit Hoskote, Penguin Books India, 2011.

Ravi Shankar: for translations 'My bones are immaterial'; 'Cool rain clouds, karuvilai blossoms'/Andal from *Post Road*, Number 22, (Boston University Journal of Literature), spring 2011.

Sampurna Chattarji: for translations 'Ma, who can comprehend your compassion' (Song 56: *Ramprasadi*); 'Mind, you never lost this delusion' (Song 69: *Ramprasadi*); 'Just try getting past me, Ma' (Song 48: *Ramprasadi)*; 'I won't be wheedled' (Song 98: *Ramprasadi*)/Ramprasad; 'Hiralal, you never went to Moti's shop' (*Hiralal Motir dokaanegelena)*; 'Mind, you don't know the gag' (*Chand dhoraphandjanona re mon*)/Lalon Fakir.

Velcheru Narayana Rao and David Shulman and Oxford University Press: for translations 'Is there some way I can reach you'; 'Lord it's up to you'; 'What can I say about my crazy ways'; 'Seeing you is one thing'; 'He's standing right next to her'; 'He's the master, what can I say'; 'Imagine I wasn't there'; 'You don't have that skill'; 'What profit will you get'; 'I am the specialist'; 'When I am done being angry'/Annamacharya; from *God on the Hill: Temple Poems from Tirupati: Annamayya,* translated by Velcheru Narayana Rao and David Shulman, Oxford University Press, 2005.

Vijay Nambisan: for translations 'Some think of name'; 'You speak of caste'/Puntanam Namboodiri from *Two Measures of Bhakti: Puntanam and Melpattur*, translated by Vijay Nambisan, Penguin Books India, 2009.

Copyright Acknowledgements

Vinay Dharwadker: for translations 'The Master Weaver'; 'Everybody understands'; 'He: neither form nor line'/Kabir from *The Weaver's Song: Kabir*, translated by Vinay Dharwadker, Penguin Books India, 2003.